WILD REVIEW

Season 2024/25

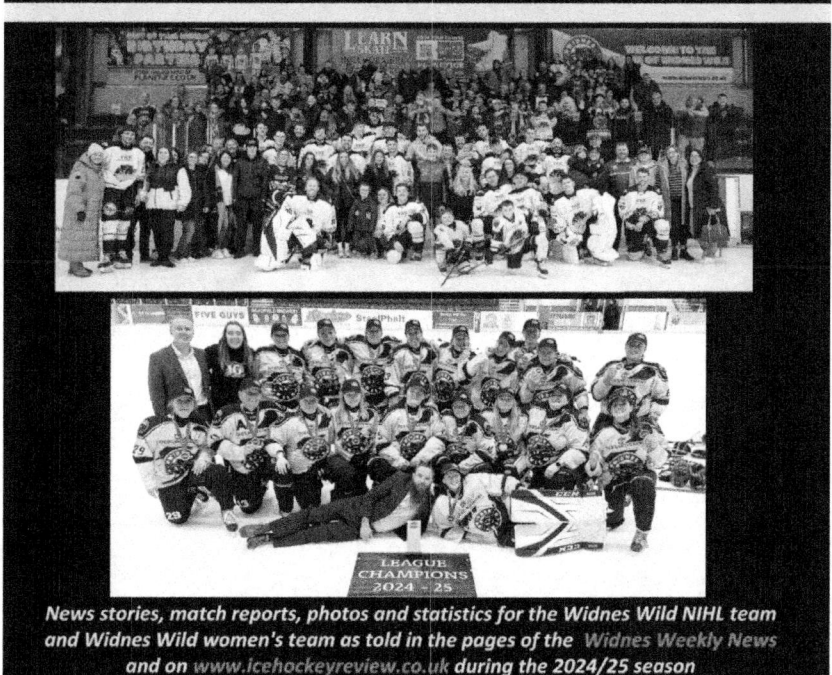

News stories, match reports, photos and statistics for the Widnes Wild NIHL team and Widnes Wild women's team as told in the pages of the Widnes Weekly News and on www.icehockeyreview.co.uk during the 2024/25 season

Interesting Books...
...Fascinating Subjects!
POSH UP NORTH
Publishing
www.poshupnorth.com

www.icehockeyreview.co.uk

Published in Great Britain in June 2025 by Ice Hockey Review
which is an imprint of Posh Up North Publishing, Beckenham Road, Wallasey

The majority of the season reviews and match reports in this book have been previously published in the Widnes Weekly News and Runcorn newspapers and on the www.icehockeyreview.co.uk.

The lists of fixtures / results, league tables and player statistics are based on information taken from EIHA gamesheets, Elite Prospects website and other sources although they have not been published anywhere in this layout before.

Intellectual rights to all works used herein remain with their originators and any perceived infringement of copyright is completely unintentional. Any errors in this regard will be corrected at the earliest possible opportunity.

British Library cataloguing in publication data.
A catalogue record for this book is available from the British Library

ISBN: 978-1-909643-69-7

Front Cover Images:
Top: The Widnes Wild NIHL team players, team staff and fans at the ent of the 2024/25 season - Photo by Steve Cunningham (Shots By Ste)

Bottom: Widnes Wild women's team – WNIHL Division 2 North Champions, May 2025 – Photo by Stewart Cutting

Back Cover Image:
Author / Editor Paul Breeze - Photo by @haganovaphoto

CONTENTS

Above: Editor Paul Breeze in the officials' box at Widnes for a Mayhem sledge game in June 2024 (Photo by Roksana Oniszczuk)

INTRODUCTION by Paul Breeze

You will notice that this year's Widnes Review book is somewhat thinner than those of previous seasons – for which I apologise, but there are reasons for this.

Basically this year's book doesn't contain anything about:

The Wild Junior Academy

The Widnes based recreational teams, or

the Mayhem Sledge team.

The Mayhem will this year be covered in a separate book that I am producing to cover the whole of the 2025 British Para Ice Hockey League, covering all of the various participating teams.

So they will still be perfectly well catered for, although that book will not be ready until September after their season has finished and the play offs have been played.

The Juniors have been doing their own match and tournament reports on their various social media outlets this season - which I am very pleased about, as they know more about what they are doing than I do – but it means that they also fall outside of the scope of this book for this year.

The Rec teams, hmmm – well.

The diplomatic way of addressing this would be to say that, over the passage of time, they don't seem to be as interested in involving me in their activities as they previously used to.

Basically – and without too much finger pointing - information hasn't been provided when I have asked for it and that makes it difficult for me to give them any media coverage through my various outlets.

Oh well, it was fun while it lasted...

But, rather than dwelling on what ISN'T in the book, let's have a look at what IS.

As with previous years, we have match by match coverage of the Widnes Wild NIHL team's Moralee Division season – with full player stats and lots of photos.

We also have match by match coverage of the Wild Women's team who won the Division 2 North league title this season!

It is fitting that they were able to win the title this season as 2025 is the 10th anniversary of the Wild Women, who were formed in the aftermath of the Manchester Phoenix fallout at Altrincham back in 2015. In a fascinating example of symmetry, they also won the league title in 2020 and as the Phoenix women's team in 2015.

People who know me will probably be aware that due to a mixture of health and personal issues, I have not been able to attend Wild matches as much as I would have liked. It is very difficult operating from a distance and much harder to keep up with what is going on when you are not in the middle of things.

Unfortunately, the "Gameday" match scoring and stats system that the EIH(A) is still insisting on foisting upon us still isn't up and running properly. From my own limited experience of it, it is very laborious to fill in, takes ages to update and is difficult to interpret once it is finished.

I maintain that most ice hockey scorers would be much happier with an actual electronic gamesheet that uses the existing format that everybody is familiar with and produces an easy to follow end document.

Colin Ellis has, in fact, devised just such a thing and it is a shame that the EIH(A) didn't adopt it and expand it for use across the leagues..

So, in view of all of this –and a few other things as well that I don't need to bother you with – I decided to stop doing week by week match reports for the Wild NIHL team at the end of this season.

It's a bit sad after having done it religiously since the start of the 2016/17 season, but life moves on - and I still have plenty to do.

There will, I'm sure, be other people at the Wild club who are just as capable of writing match reports as I am and I look forward to seeing their work in the future.

I will still be reporting on the Wild Women's team and the Mayhem sledge team – whose matches I find it easier to get to – so you won't be getting rid of me all together, and I will still be following the fortunes of the Wild NIHL in a more general manner.

And, as ever, you can keep up with all the various things that I am covering on my website:

www.icehockeyreview.co.uk

So, in closing, what you have here is the best summary of the ice hockey played at Widnes during the 2024/25 season that I can muster – bearing in mind all the usual turmoil behind the scenes.

I hope you find it interesting and enjoyable.

Paul

.

NIHL Moralee Division – Season 2024/25

Final Table	GP	W	OTW	OTL	L	GF	GA	Pts
Billingham Stars	36	33	0	0	3	260	88	99
Blackburn Hawks	36	29	1	0	6	242	104	89
Solihull Barons	36	23	2	1	10	220	152	74
Deeside Dragons	36	19	3	0	14	210	204	63
Hull Jets	36	18	1	5	12	149	129	61
Whitley Warriors	36	17	0	1	18	151	156	52
Nottingham Lions	36	13	1	1	21	156	173	42
Leeds Knights	36	6	1	3	26	109	215	23
Widnes Wild	36	6	2	0	28	119	232	22
Sheffield Scimitars	36	4	1	1	30	78	244	15

Top Points Scorers

Player	Team	GP	G	A	Pts	PIM
Niklas Ottosson	Solihull Barons	33	37	80	117	8
Jake Witkowski	Deeside Dragons	30	52	58	110	51
Daniel Mulcahy	Solihull Barons	35	50	60	110	18
Iain Brown	Billingham Stars	35	68	35	103	22
Chris Sykes	Billingham Stars	36	29	74	103	31
Michael Elder	Billingham Stars	35	28	59	87	16
Philip Edgar	Whitley Warriors	24	34	43	77	41
Jacob Lutwyche	Blackburn Hawks	34	47	28	75	6
Alex Rushby	Nottingham Lions	32	33	42	75	4
Adam Barnes	Blackburn Hawks	35	40	34	74	10

Top Netminders

Netminder	Team	GPI	Mins	SA	GA	GAA	SV%	SO
Mark Turnbull	BIL	12	648	320	24	2.13	92.50%	1
Jacob Hammond	BIL	25	1453	761	61	2.52	92.00%	1
Zack Brown	HUL	24	1456	916	77	3.17	91.60%	1
Oliver Thomasson	BLA	17	900	426	36	2.40	91.50%	1
Ben Keddie	BLA	22	1260	694	67	3.19	90.30%	3
Luca Sheldon	NOT	10	485	303	31	3.84	89.80%	0
Harry Campbell	WID	21	1248	928	103	4.95	88.90%	0
Joshua Crane	WHI	22	1231	791	91	4.44	88.50%	0

Widnes Wild players, team staff, match volunteers and fans celebrate the home win against Nottingham in the last game of the season. (Photo by Steve Cunningham)

Widnes Wild NIHL Season Review

The Widnes Wild NIHL team had a difficult 2024/25 season in the NIHL Moralee Division, finishing in 9th place in the league table and winning just 8 of their 36 league games.

However, this really needs putting into perspective.

The team had only managed 7th place in the Moralee Division table the previous season and 7 of their 8 top points scorers for the 2023/24 campaign moved on to pastures new during the summer. Tom Jackson was newly installed as Head Coach and a number of new faces were brought into the squad – all of which would take some time to gel.

The club readily admitted at the start of the season that this was to be a year of rebuilding and it proved to be quite a steep learning curve for all involved.

9

The season started with a 9-game losing streak that saw the Wild mired at the bottom of the Moralee Division league table. An over time win away at fellow strugglers Sheffield Scimitars and a morale boosting victory away to local rivals Deeside Dragons showed that the potential was there but it took until 22nd December for Widnes to record their first home win – a 12-4 victory over Sheffield.

The performances certainly improved over the course of the season, although the results didn't always reflect that. The margins of defeat became narrower and a few hard fought wins over other teams around the bottom of the table saw Widnes finally climb above Sheffield and escape the "wooden spoon" spot of 10th place.

Matty Barlow came back from an unhappy stint at Leeds Knights in November and the roster was further boosted prior to the signing deadline by the return of Flynn Massie and Dani Haid.

The upturn in form, coupled with the vagaries of the fixture list - which saw four potentially winnable games against Nottingham in the latter half of the season and two against Leeds who were just above Widnes in the 8th and final play off place – meant that the Wild now had a realistic target to aim for.

They lost away to Nottingham at the end of February but an exciting run of three wins in their last three homes game of the season – once against Leeds and twice over the Lions - saw them finish an agonisingly close single point behind Leeds and just out of the play-offs.

In terms of individual player statistics, Mikey Gilbert was the Wild's top points scorer for the season overall with 16 goals and 33 assists in 34 games. Team captain Andrew

Hopkins was the top goal scorer with 22 strikes and he was the only Wild player to play in all 36 league games.

Matty Barlow was second highest goalscorer with 18, which is all the more impressive as he only played in 24 matches, and Bailey Thomson also reached double figures with 13 goals in 23 games.

In term of penalties, Damarni James finished up as the leader in the Wild's "Bad Boy" stakes with 107 penalty minutes from his 26 games, picking up a few EIH suspensions for his troubles. Ben McLellan weighed in at a distant second with 80 PIMs.

Probably the most promising aspect of the Wild's up and down season has been the fact that a number of younger players have had the opportunity to establish themselves as regular players at NIHL Moralee Division level.

17 year old Wild Academy junior player Luke Alston played in 33 of the Wild's league games, scoring 9 goals and 6 assists, seeing him finish as their 5th highest scorer overall for the season.

Getting quality ice time and big game experience is an essential part of a young player's development and, taking full advantage of the rules that were put in place that encourage this, Alston has also played this season with Bradford Bulldogs in the NIHL Laidler Division, Kilmarnock Thunder in the Scottish National League, Kilmarnock Avalanche in the Scottish U19 league and the Wild Academy Under 18 team.

It's a similar story with Jared Knowles, who played 21 times for the Wild in his senior "breakout" season, contributing 4 assists. He also played for Bradford Bulldogs and the Wild Under 18 team.

Another graduate of the Wild Academy, Joel Bark, played 5 Moralee Division NIHL games for the Wild on a 2-way with Bradford while 18 year old Kai Hathaway - a former Manchester Storm junior – played 20 games for the Wild scoring 4 goals, and also had successful spells with the Bulldogs and the Wild Under 19 team.

19 year old netminder Harry Campbell was the most impressive of the 5 netminders used over the course of the season, picking up numerous MVP awards for his efforts in Wild games, playing on a 2-way deal and splitting his time between Widnes and Kilmarnock Thunder in the SNL.

Mikey Gilbert was the Wild's top points scorer of the season. (Photo by Keith & Jenny Davies)

Jared Knowles (Photo by David Tattum)

Luke Alston (Photo by Keith & Jenny Davies)

Widnes Wild Fixtures & Results – Season 2024/25

Date	Com	Home			Away	WDL
01/09/2024	Ch	Widnes Wild	12	2	Bradford Bulldogs	W
07/09/2024	Ch	Widnes Wild	3	5	Telford Tigers	L
08/09/2024	Ch	Telford Tigers	4	1	Widnes Wild	L
14/09/2024	L*	Hull Jets	9	2	Widnes Wild	L
15/09/2024	L*	Widnes Wild	3	6	Billingham Stars	L
22/09/2024	L*	Widnes Wild	2	7	Deeside Dragons	L
29/09/2024	L*	Widnes Wild	2	7	Leeds Knights	L
05/10/2024	L*	Leeds Knights	5	2	Widnes Wild	L
06/10/2024	L*	Whitley Warriors	9	2	Widnes Wild	L
13/10/2024	L*	Widnes Wild	3	8	Solihull Barons	L
20/10/2024	L*	Widnes Wild	2	16	Blackburn Hawks	L
27/10/2024	L*	Widnes Wild	1	3	Hull Jets	L
02/11/2024	L*	Sheffield Scims	3	3	Widnes Wild	WOT
03/11/2024	L*	Billingham Stars	7	0	Widnes Wild	L
10/11/2024	L	Widnes Wild	4	7	Whitley Warriors	L
16/11/2024	L	Billingham Stars	15	2	Widnes Wild	L
17/11/2024	L	Widnes Wild	2	5	Sheffield Scims	L
24/11/2024	L	Deeside Dragons	4	5	Widnes Wild	W
01/12/2024	L	Widnes Wild	1	4	Whitley Warriors	L
07/12/2024	L	Solihull Barons	8	2	Widnes Wild	L
14/12/2024	L	Sheffield Scims	1	4	Widnes Wild	W
15/12/2024	L	Blackburn Hawks	7	1	Widnes Wild	L
21/12/2024	L	Widnes Wild	4	10	Deeside Dragons	L
22/12/2024	L	Widnes Wild	12	4	Sheffield Scims	W
11/01/2025	L	Leeds Knights	7	2	Widnes Wild	L
12/01/2025	L	Widnes Wild	5	7	Solihull Barons	L
18/01/2025	L	Nottingham Lions	3	5	Widnes Wild	W
25/01/2025	L	Widnes Wild	2	6	Blackburn Hawks	L
01/02/2025	L	Widnes Wild	2	4	Hull Jets	L
08/02/2025	L	Blackburn Hawks	8	2	Widnes Wild	L
09/02/2025	L	Widnes Wild	1	3	Billingham Stars	L
16/02/2025	L	Solihull Barons	12	5	Widnes Wild	L
22/02/2025	L	Deeside Dragons	9	8	Widnes Wild	L
23/02/2025	L	Nottingham Lions	6	2	Widnes Wild	L
02/03/2025	L	Widnes Wild	5	4	Leeds Knights	WOT
08/03/2025	L	Widnes Wild	8	4	Nottingham Lions	W
15/03/2025	L	Whitley Warriors	3	1	Widnes Wild	L
16/03/2025	L	Hull Jets	7	5	Widnes Wild	L
22/03/2025	L	Widnes Wild	7	5	Nottingham Lions	W

Note: matches count towards both league and cup qualification group*

14

Widnes Wild Player Statistics - 2024/25
Moralee Division Only

Player	GP	G	A	Pts	PIM
Michael Gilbert	34	16	33	49	8
Andy Hopkins	36	22	17	39	37
Matt Barlow	24	18	16	34	38
Bailey Thomson	23	13	13	26	38
Luke Alston	33	9	6	15	2
Ben McLellan	30	3	12	15	80
Daniel Haid	13	7	7	14	0
Tomas Vyrostek	27	6	8	14	26
Ross Chalmers	15	3	10	13	10
Flynn Massie	13	3	9	12	6
Jonathon Williamson	33	2	10	12	18
Damarni James	26	5	5	10	107
Bez Hughes	34	2	7	9	22
Joe Howie	32	1	7	8	12
Owen Rae	19	2	5	7	22
Kai Hathaway	20	4	0	4	2
Jared Knowles	21	0	4	4	50
Matt Tarpey	24	1	2	3	6
Harry Campbell	21	0	2	2	2
Will Daley	21	0	2	2	4
Nathan Pollard	1	1	0	1	0
Robbie Thomson	7	1	0	1	4
Scott Kirkpatrick	18	0	1	1	18
Andrew Craik	19	0	0	0	6
Logan Reid	14	0	0	0	0
Jake Lowndes	6	0	0	0	0
Joel Bark	5	0	0	0	0
Samuel Wojcik	2	0	0	0	0
Charlie Henry	7	0	0	0	0
Paul Maudsley	22	0	0	0	0
Bench					8

Netminder	GPI	Mins	SA	GA	GAA	SV%	SO
Harry Campbell	21	1247	928	103	4.95	88.90%	0
Logan Reid	11	515	400	70	8.16	82.50%	0
Charlie Henry	5	170	114	24	8.47	78.90%	0
Paul Maudsley	3	137	129	19	8.31	85.30%	0
Jake Lowndes	2	88	66	14	9.48	78.80%	0

Widnes Wild Player Statistics - 2024/25
Challenge Matches Only

Player	GP	G	A	Pts	PIM
Andy Hopkins	3	2	4	6	0
Jared Knowles	3	3	2	5	0
Tristan Grimshaw	1	1	3	4	0
Damarni James	3	3	2	4	2
Matt Tarpey	3	2	2	4	0
Michael Gilbert	3	1	2	3	2
Andrew Craik	3	2	1	3	0
Ross Chalmers	2	2	0	2	0
Luke Alston	3	0	2	2	2
Jonathon Williamson	3	0	1	1	0
Bailey Thomson	1	0	0	0	0
Kai Hathaway	1	0	0	0	0
Harry Campbell	1	0	0	0	0
Robbie Thomson	1	0	0	0	2
Joel Bark	1	0	0	0	0
Will Daley	2	0	0	0	0
Scott Kirkpatrick	2	0	0	0	2
Logan Reid	2	0	0	0	0
Bez Hughes	3	0	0	0	0
Joe Howie	3	0	0	0	0
Charlie Henry	3	0	0	0	0

Match	Netminder	GPI	Mins	SA	GA	GAA	Sv%
V BRD	Harry Campbell	1	60.00	27	2	2.00	92.59
V TEL	Charlie Henry	1	59.53	49	5	5.00	89.80
@ TEL	Logan Reid*	1	60.00	49	4	4.00	91.84

Note: player assists and PIMs stats are incomplete for the away game at Telford.   * = estimated NM figures.

Widnes Wild Player Statistics - 2024/25
All Games (Moralee Division & Challenge Matches)

Player	GP	G	A	Pts	PIM
Michael Gilbert	37	17	35	52	10
Andy Hopkins	39	24	21	45	37
Matt Barlow	24	18	16	34	38
Bailey Thomson	24	13	13	26	38
Luke Alston	36	9	8	17	4
Ben McLellan	30	3	12	15	80
Ross Chalmers	17	5	10	15	10
Damarni James	29	8	7	14	109
Tomas Vyrostek	27	6	8	14	26
Daniel Haid	13	7	7	14	0
Jonathon Williamson	36	2	11	13	18
Flynn Massie	13	3	9	12	6
Bez Hughes	37	2	7	9	22
Jared Knowles	24	3	6	9	50
Joe Howie	35	1	7	8	12
Matt Tarpey	27	3	4	7	6
Owen Rae	19	2	5	7	22
Kai Hathaway	21	4	0	4	2
Tristan Grimshaw	1	1	3	4	0
Andrew Craik	22	2	1	3	6
Will Daley	23	0	2	2	4
Harry Campbell	22	0	2	2	2
Scott Kirkpatrick	20	0	1	1	20
Robbie Thomson	8	1	0	1	6
Nathan Pollard	1	1	0	1	0
Paul Maudsley	22	0	0	0	0
Logan Reid	16	0	0	0	0
Charlie Henry	10	0	0	0	0
Jake Lowndes	6	0	0	0	0
Joel Bark	6	0	0	0	0
Samuel Wojcik	2	0	0	0	0
Bench	0	0	0	0	8

Netminder	Comp	GPI	Mins	SA	GA	GAA	SV%
Harry Campbell	Lge	21	1247	928	103	4.95	88.90
Harry Campbell	Cha	1	60	27	2	2	92.59
	Totals	22	1307	955	105	4.82	89.01
Logan Reid	Lge	11	515	400	70	8.16	82.50
Logan Reid*	Cha	1	60	49	4	4	91.84
	Totals	12	575	449	74	7.72	83.52
Charlie Henry	Lge	5	170	114	24	8.47	78.90
Charlie Henry	Cha	1	59.53	49	5	5	89.8
	Totals	6	229.53	163	29	7.58	82.21
Paul Maudsley	Lge	3	137	129	19	8.31	85.30
Jake Lowndes	Lge	2	88	66	14	9.48	78.80

Tom Jackson is the new Widnes Wild NIHL Player Coach
(Photo by David Tattum / DJT Ice Hockey Photos)

Tom Jackson Appointed Widnes Wild Player Coach

The Widnes Wild NIHL team have announced that popular senior player Tom Jackson has been appointed Player/Coach for the forthcoming 2024/25 Moralee Division season.

The team's longest serving player has been team captain for the past 3 seasons and has taken on the new role following the departure of Joey Coulter, who has decided to leave the club after 1½ seasons in charge.

Jackson joined the Wild midway through their debut 2013/14 season, having played his junior hockey at Hull, and in the intervening 11 years has made 312 appearances in Widnes colours, scoring 17 goals, 70 assists and picking up 389 penalty minutes.

Talking about his appointment, Jackson said:

"When I heard Joey was moving on I was gutted! Joey isn't just a coach - he's a good friend to the guys in the locker room, so finding out he's moving on was a big shock to the system.

After speaking to him about his decision, we discussed the idea of me taking over and that's now becoming a reality. It's a role in which I will be learning as I go, but I'm open to the challenge ahead of me and I want to build the team around the values I have for the future, not just the here and now."

"Widnes is the place I've called home since an 18 year old boy coming into the game of senior hockey. It's a place where I've felt both success and failure throughout that time, which is part of the fun of ice hockey.

My goal is to spend as long coaching as I have playing here and to build something for both the future of the club, and for the fans of old and new to enjoy."

Andrew Craik scored on his Wild debut
(Photo by Keith & Jenny Davies)

Sunday 1st September 2024 – Challenge Match
Widnes Wild 12 – Bradford Bulldogs 2

The Widnes Wild NIHL team got the new season off to a winning start with a comprehensive 12-2 victory over Bradford Bulldogs on Sunday at Planet Ice Widnes.

The Bulldogs are a Laidler Division side - and play one division below the Wild – so one can't really read too much into the result of this pre-season friendly match but it was certainly a good first outing for Player Coach Tom Jackson's new look Widnes team and it gave fans the chance to see all the new signings together on the ice.

The game saw an unprecedented number of Wild debuts handed out, following a busy summer of player movements, with 9 brand new names featuring on the roster. Forwards Kai Hathaway, Robbie Thomson & Andrew Craik, defencemen Ross Chalmers, William Daley, Joe Howie & Scott Kirkpatrick and netminders Charlie Henry & Harry Campbell all made first appearances in Wild colours.

Widnes Academy junior player Jared Knowles made his first senior appearance for the club while former Wild players Tristan Grimshaw and Matt Tarpey both returned to the team after a number of seasons away. The Bradford team also looked quite familiar as former Wild players Jake Lowndes, Tom Mardell, Keiron Fulrong and Joel Bark were all on the Bulldogs line up.

Despite so many new faces playing together for the first time, the new look Widnes team seemed to gel very well. Damarni James scored the first goal of the new season in the second minute and the Wild raced into a 6-0 lead by the end of the first period with further goals from James (again), Knowles, Grimshaw, Tarpey and Craik.

The second period saw goals from Mikey Gilbert, Andrew Hopkins and Chalmers and the third, Chalmers Knowles and Tarpey for a 12-2 win.

The Wild will probably face a tougher test this coming weekend when they have a home and away double header against last season's Laidler Division champions Telford Tigers.

 The home game is on Saturday 7th September, 7pm face off, and the away game is the next day in Telford, with the puck dropping at 6pm.

New Wild Captain Andrew Hopkins with Bez Hughes (left) and Jonathan Williamson (right) - Photo by Steve Cunningham

Captains Aboard

Prior to the home game against Bradford, the Wild NIHL team unveiled their captaincy team for the 2024/25 season.

Andrew Hopkins is the team captain for the new season, taking over the role that was vacated by Tom Jackson when he was appointed player coach during the summer. The Alternate Captain roles (AC) go to Bez Hughes and Jonathan Williamson. The role of Alternate Captain is very important because, in ice hockey, only the Captain is allowed to discuss decisions with the match referee.

If the Team Captain is on the bench at the time of the call, he is not allowed to rush onto the ice to query it and, therefore, each playing line has an Alternate Captain to ensure that this role is always covered throughout the game.

After Jackson, Bez Hughes is the Wild's longest serving player, having originally joined for the 2014/15 season.

Jared Knowles (Photo by Steve Cunningham)

Saturday 7th September – Challenge Match
Widnes Wild 3 – Telford Tigers 5

Sunday 8th September – Challenge Match
Telford Tigers 4 - Widnes Wild 1

The Widnes Wild NIHL team had a disappointing weekend with back to back defeats at the hands of last season's Laidler Division champions Telford Tigers, losing 3-5 at home on Saturday and 4-1 away on Sunday.

The home game on Saturday saw a rather depleted Wild line up compared with the three full lines that had battered Bradford Bulldogs the week before but they managed to take a 2-0 lead in the first 10 minutes with goals from new team captain Andrew Hopkins and former Solway Sharks and Edinburgh Capitals player Andrew Craik, who joined the Wild during the summer.

Telford pulled a goal back to bring the score to 2-1 at the first break and then scored two unanswered goals in the second period to lead 2-3 after 40 minutes of play.

Outstanding Wild youngster Jared Knowles equalised two minutes into the third period with his third goal in two games for Widnes but two more goals – including an empty net strike after netminder Charlie Henry had been taken off in favour of an extra attacker - secured the win for the Tigers.

The away game on Sunday was pretty close in its early stages but Telford eventually took the lead on 15 minutes. They doubled the advantage 90 seconds into the second period and Widnes finally opened their own account with a Damarni James goal on 26 minutes.

A penalty shot early in the third period edged the Tigers further ahead again and a goal from former Wild import Filip Supa rounded off the scoring for the game with 10 minutes left to play.

The NIHL season proper starts this weekend with a road trip to Hull and back this Saturday 14th September when the Wild play Hull Jets in their first league fixture of the season. They are home on Sunday when they take on last season's league champions Billingham Stars at Planet Ice Widnes, 5.30pm face off.

Widnes Academy players who have joined the Wild NIHL team for the 2024/25 season - #12 Luke Alston, #19 Jared Knowles, #6 Kai Hathaway and #64 Robbie Thomson – along with coaches Mikey Gilbert and Gary Eddleston (Photo by Steve Cunningham)

The #64 Shirt Mystery Unravelled

Eagle-eyed Widnes fans will have noticed that the #64 shirt has been in evidence again at Wild matches this season.

The number 64 was previously worn by original Wild netminder Greg Ruxton who played in the very first in Widnes game back in August 2013 and stayed with the club for four seasons from 2013 to 2017.

Ruxton was forced to give up playing due to a recurring knee injury and his career at the Wild was recognised with a special on-ice ceremony in October 2017, which also saw his #64 shirt "retired".

Commenting on the resurrection of the #64 shirt, Wild GM Steve Cunningham explained: "We spoke to Greg and he is happy to honour the number and not retire it."

Kai Hathaway scored the first Wild goal against Deeside
(Photo by David Tattum)

Sunday 22nd September – Moralee Division
Widnes Wild 2 – Deeside Dragons 7

The Widnes Wild NIHL team's disappointing start to the season continued with a 2-7 defeat at the hands of local rivals Deeside Dragons at Planet Ice Widnes on Sunday.

Due to the close proximity of the two teams – and regular interchanges of players over the years - matches with the Dragons are always feisty affairs and this was no exception.

Am alarmingly short-benched Widnes actually scored first with a goal by Kai Hathaway but three strikes for the Dragons – including a brace from former Wild favourite Jakub Hajek - saw the visitors leading 1-3 at the first period break.

27

Luke Alston narrowed the deficit to just one goal midway through the second period but two goals late on handed the Dragons a 2-5 lead with one period left to play.

The game was pretty much dominated by Deeside's new import and former Leeds Knights National Division player - American Jake Witowksy – and he rounded off an impressive hat trick to go with his three assists to bring the score to 2-6 midway through the third period.

A seventh goal for the Dragons late in the game further rubbed salt in the Wild wounds and bragging rights remain at the western end of the M56 – at least until the next Widnes / Deeside encounter.

The Wild are next in action this Sunday 29th September when they are at home to the new Leeds Knights 2 team in the Moralee Division at Planet Ice Widnes, 5.30pm face off.

Jonathan Williamson was the Wild NIHL team's MVP against Leeds
(Photo by Keith & Jenny Davies)

Sunday 29th September 2024 – NIHL Moralee Division
Widnes Wild 2 – Leeds Knights 7

The Widnes Wild NIHL team lost their 4th league game in a row with a 2-7 defeat at the hands of Leeds Knights at Planet Ice Widnes on Sunday.

The Leeds Knights NIHL 1 team are new to the Moralee Division this year and they have assembled an impressive roster that includes three overseas born players – among them a US AAA trained junior - as well as Matty Barlow and Alex Mitchell, who both played for Widnes for the past two seasons.

This cross-Pennine derby game was niggly from the off and was littered with minor penalties throughout. The only goal of the first period came on 13 minutes and it fell to the visitors who took the 0-1 lead into the first interval.

Bailey Thomson equalised for the Wild on 28 minutes but Barlow fired the Knights back in front just 30 seconds later. 2 more goals put Leeds further ahead and they led 1-4 at the second period break.

The Knights went 1-5 up just 36 seconds into the third period but Jono Williamson pulled a goal back for Widnes 3 minutes later. However, this wasn't enough to spark a late revival and two more goals for Leeds late on made the score look a little more one-sided than the game actually was.

It was Leeds' first win of the season after 4 straight defeats and the result leaves Widnes and Sheffield both adrift at the bottom of the Moralee Division table, still looking for their first points.

The Wild have back to back away games at the weekend when they play away to Leeds on Saturday 5th October and then make the long trip to the North East to take on Whitley Warriors on Sunday.

They are next at home on Sunday 13th October when they take on Solihull Barons at Planet Ice Widnes, 5.30pm face off.

Matt Tarpey (Photo by Keith & Jenny Davies)

Saturday 5th October 2020 – NIHL Moralee Division
Leeds Knights 5 – Widnes Wild 2

Sunday 6th October 2024 – NIHL Moralee Division
Whitley Warriors 9 – Widnes Wild 2

The Widnes Wild NIHL team's disappointing start to the season continued with back to back away defeats – 5-2 at Leeds Knights on Saturday and 9-2 away to Whitley Warriors on Sunday.

The weekend saw a Widnes debut for 16 year old Tomas Vyrostek, who is a Solway Sharks junior player with Scottish international honours, and the return of a number of 2-way players to the team, but this – sadly – it wasn't enough to change the fortunes of the struggling Wild side.

In the game in Leeds on Saturday, Widnes actually took the lead with a goal from Bailey Thomson in the 6th minute but they were then pegged back to 1-1 at the first period break. Two unanswered goals in the second period saw the Knights edge into the lead and two more goals early in the third put them well in control.

Matt Tarpey pulled a goal back for the Wild with just 62 seconds left on the clock but it was too late in the game to spark a fightback and the match ended 5-2 to Leeds.

Away games in the north east are always tough affairs but Widnes fared quite well in the early stages of the match at Whitley on Sunday and the score was 1-1 after the first period, courtesy of a Wild goal from Mikey Gilbert.

Unfortunately, 6 unanswered goals in the second period put paid to any hopes of the Wild bringing any points home from this lengthy road trip - and a second Gilbert goal in the third period was pretty much the only other thing for the travelling fans to cheer about in the resulting 9-2 defeat.

The weekend results mean that the Wild are still looking for their first league win of the season, with 6 straight defeats under their belts. They are joined at the bottom of the Moralee Division table by Sheffield Scimitars who also have "nul –points" after having lost 8 from 8 starts.

Widnes will be hoping to kick-start their season with a win this Sunday 13th October when they take on Solihull Barons at Planet Ice Widnes, 5.30pm face off.

Sunday 13th October 2024 – NIHL Laidler Division
Widnes Wild 3 – Solihull Barons 8

The Widnes Wild NIHL team put in a spirited performance against the Solihull Barons but it wasn't enough to prevent them slumping to a 3-8 defeat at Planet Ice Widnes on Sunday.

The Wild started the game well and actually took the lead with a goal from Jonathan Williamson after 5 minutes but were pegged back and trailed 1-2 at the first period break.

A third goal for Solihull just 31 seconds into the second period saw the visitors edge further ahead but Widnes struck back and a goal from Damarni James narrowed the deficit back to just one. A successfully converted penalty shot on 33 minutes saw the Barons re-establish their two-goal lead and the score stood at 2-4 at the second interval.

Two more goals for Solihull early in the third period effectively put paid to any hopes of a late Widnes fightback and a seventh goal on 50 minutes simply confirmed their superiority.

Team Captain Andrew Hopkins fired in a third goal for Widnes just 25 seconds after that - but that was the last thing that the home fans got to cheer about and the Barons piled on the misery with an eighth goal of their own with just over a minute left to play.

The result extends the Wild's losing streak to 7 defeats in a row for this Moralee Division season and you have to go right back to February for their last competitive win – when they beat Sheffield Scimitars in over time.

A surprise win at the weekend for the struggling Scimitars away at early season league leaders Hull Jets saw them leapfrog the Wild off the bottom of the league table, leaving Widnes as the only team without a point so far this season.

 Widnes will be hoping to bounce straight back from this latest setback when they take on fierce rivals Blackburn Hawks in their next game – a tantalising north west derby - this Sunday 20th October at Planet Ice Widnes, 5.30pm face off.

Sunday 20th October 2024 – NIHL Laidler Division
Widnes Wild 2 – Blackburn Hawks 16

The Widnes Wild NIHL team suffered a disappointing 2-16 defeat at the hands of North West rivals Blackburn Hawks at Planet Ice Widnes on Sunday.

Blackburn were the better team throughout this game and took the lead just 90 seconds into the first period. They led 0-5 at the first period break and scored three more goals before Widnes finally managed to find the net themselves.

A well taken strike in the top corner of the net from Bailey Thomson broke the Wild duck on 38 minutes and then a first goal for the club from Tomas Vyrostek just 90 seconds later sparked faint hopes of a Widnes fightback.

However, that was as good as things got for the Wild fans and the score stubbornly remained 2-8 at the second interval. Eight unanswered goals for the Hawks piled on the misery in the third period and the Wild slumped to their heaviest defeat of the season.

Having lost all 8 of their league games so far this season, the Wild will be hoping for a change of fortune when they face high-flying Hull Jets in their next game this Sunday 27th October at Planet Ice Widnes, 5.30pm face off.

Sunday 27th October 2024 – NIHL Laidler Division
Widnes Wild 1 – Hull Jets 3

The Widnes Wild NIHL team's winless start to the season continued with a 1-3 defeat at home to high flying Hull Jets at Planet Ice Widnes on Sunday.

While a defeat is always disappointing, compared to the last league game - where the Wild conceded a record 16 goals at home to Blackburn - this was a much better all round performance and suggests that there may be light at the end of the tunnel.

There was little to choose between the two teams in this game and Widnes were in with a shout until the very end.

Hull took the lead on 5 minutes but Tomas Vyrostek equalised 7 minutes later and the score stood at a very respectable 1-1 at the first period break.

A goal from former Wild player coach Richard Haggar edged the Jets ahead once again at the midway point of the game but that was the only strike of the second period and there was still plenty for both sides to play for in the final 20 minutes.

The Jets extended their lead with a goal just 1 minute into the third period and try, as they might, Widnes were unable to find a way past the stubborn Hull defence. The clock ticked down and the score remained 1-3 at the final buzzer.

Having lost all 9 of their league games so far this season, the Wild will be hoping for a change of fortunes when they face fellow strugglers Sheffield Scimitars away at iceSheffield this Saturday 2nd November, 4.20pm face off.

They then face a long trip to the north east to face league leaders Billingham Stars on Sunday – 5.30pm start.

Saturday 2nd November 2024 – NIHL Moralee Division
Sheffield Scimitars 2 - Widnes Wild 3 (OTW)

Sunday 3rd November 2024 – NIHL Moralee Division
Billingham Stars 7 - Widnes Wild 0

The Widnes Wild NIHL team had a mixed weekend on the road, winning 2-3 in overtime away to Sheffield Scimitars on Saturday and then losing 7-0 away to league leaders Billingham Stars on Sunday.

The win away in Sheffield over fellow strugglers Scimitars was the Wild's first league win of the season and was especially welcome as it removed the spectre that had been looming of notching up 10 league defeats in a row for the first time in one season.

As you can imagine from the scoreline, the game was very closely fought throughout and the result could easily have gone either way.

The Scimitars scored first and led 1-0 at the first interval and then scored again early in the second period. A goal from Wild captain Andrew Hopkins halved the deficit and the score stood at a finely poised 2-1 at the second period break.

A first goal for the Wild from recent signing Ben Mclellan tied the score at 2-2 and sent the game into a nail-biting overtime period where Jonathan Williamson fired in the sudden death winner.

Under new regulations introduced for this season, Widnes receive 2 league points for the overtime win while Sheffield get 1 point for drawing at the end of regulation time.

The game on Sunday away to league leaders and defending champions Billingham Stars was always going to be difficult, and so it turned out. The Stars led 2-0 at the end of the first period, 4-0 at the end of the second and then a third period hat-trick from their Canadian star Iain Brown rounded off the scoring for a 7-0 shut out.

The Wild are next in action this Sunday 10th November whey they take on Whitley Warriors at Planet Ice Widnes, 5.30pm face off.

The teams laid poppy wreaths on the ice before the game on Remembrance Sunday (Photo by David Tattum)

Sunday 10th November 2024 – NIHL Moralee Division Widnes Wild 4 – Whitley Warriors 7

The Widnes Wild NIHL team put in a battling performance in the Remembrance Day game before losing out 4-7 to Whitley Warriors in the NIHL Moralee Division at Planet Ice Widnes on Sunday.

The game was very close in its early stages and the Wild took the lead through team captain Andrew Hopkins and held the 1-0 advantage at the first interval.

Widnes had the chance to go 2-0 up on 26 minutes when Matty Barlow was brought down on a breakaway and was awarded a Penalty Shot - but the Warriors netminder saved and the score remained 1-0. Boosted by the this, the Warriors scored their first goal just 20 seconds later and then went 1-2 up on 32 minutes.

Two quick-fire goals within 40 seconds of each other – from Mikey Gilbert and Hopkins again – saw the Wild draw level and re-take the lead but two counter-strikes late in the period saw Whitley leading 3-4 at the second break.

A shorthanded goal from Damarni James just 58 seconds into the third period drew Widnes level once again but Whitley upped their game and two goals from Shaun Kippin put daylight between the two teams for the first time with 8 minutes left to play.

With time agonisingly ticking by, the Wild withdrew netminder Harry Campbell in favour of an extra attacker for the closing minutes to try and narrow the two goal deficit in the for the closing minutes. Defenceman Will Daley kept them in the game with a dramatic goal line clearance but an Empty Net Goal from Whitley's Kippin to secure his hat-trick rounded off the scoring with just 38 seconds left on the clock.

The Wild are away to league leaders Billingham Stars this Saturday 16th November in a re-arranged fixture and are next at home on Sunday 17th November when they take on Sheffield Scimitars at Planet Ice Widnes, 5.30pm face off.

Tomas Vyrostek (Photo by Keith & Jenny Davies)

Vyrostek Signs For Season

The Widnes Wild NIHL team have signed Tomas Vyrostek on a permanent basis for the rest of the season.

Tomas originally joined the Wild on a temporary basis having progressed through the Solway Sharks academy, racking up an impressive 73 points from 27 games at Under 16 level and 35 points across his 2 seasons at Under level so far. He has also represented Scotland at Under 16 and Under 17 level, posting 5 points from 10 games.

Vyrostek made his debut last season in the Scottish National League (SNL) with the North Ayrshire Wild and also made multiple appearances for the Solway Sharks NIHL team during pre-season.

However, this season is his first experience of playing Moralee Division hockey, where he has already made a huge impact with Widnes, scoring 3 goals in 9 appearances - including the all-important game winning overtime goal away at Sheffield to help secure the Wild's first league victory of the season.

Saturday 16th November – NIHL Moralee Division
Billingham Stars 15 – Widnes Wild 2

Sunday 17th November – NIHL Moralee Division
Widnes Wild 2 – Sheffield Scimitars 5

The Widnes Wild NIHL team had a disappointing weekend with back to back defeats, losing 15-2 away to Billingham Stars on Saturday and then 2-5 at home to Sheffield Scimitars on Sunday at Planet Ice Widnes.

The away trip to the North East to face the league leaders was always going to be a tough one and the Wild were outplayed pretty much from the start.

The first period ended 5-1 to the home team, with a solitary strike from Bailey Thomson being just enough to keep Widnes in the running. By the end of the second period, the score was 10-2 – with Mikey Gilbert adding to the Wild total - and then 5 unanswered goals for the Stars in the third saw them romp to an emphatic victory.

Sunday's home game against fellow strugglers Sheffield looked to be considerably more winnable but a short benched Widnes – missing a number of key players – never really managed to get going.

After a tense opening spell, the Scimitars opened the scoring in the 15th minute and led 0-2 at the first interval.

This game was littered with niggly penalties for both sides and Widnes seemed unable to build up any kind of momentum. The only goal of the second period fell to former Wild player George Crawshaw and the score stood at 0-3 with 20 minutes left to play.

Mikey Gilbert gave the home fans some hope with a Widnes goal 2 minutes into the third period but Sheffield struck back to re-establish the three goal cushion.

Matty Barlow fired in his first goal since returning to the Wild for his third spell last week to narrow the score to 2-4 but Widnes got caught out while pushing forward to try and salvage something from the game and a 5th goal for the visitors late on killed off any lingering hopes.

The weekend results leave the Wild languishing at the bottom of the Moralee Division table with just 2 points from their 14 league games to date. Leeds Knights are in 9th place - 5 points ahead, having played the same number of games.

The Wild are away to local rivals Deeside Dragons this Sunday 24th November - 5.15pm - face off and are next at home on Sunday 1st December when they take on Whitley Warriors at Planet Ice Widnes, 5.30pm face off.

Matty Barlow Returns To The Wild

The Widnes Wild NIHL team have announced that popular forward Matty Barlow has rejoined the club for the rest of the season.

This is actually Barlow's third stint with Widnes as he played 32 games as part of Ollie Barron's Laidler Division play off winning team in 2017/18 and then spent a further 3 seasons at Widnes in the post-covid Moralee Division from 2021 to 2024.

He moved to join the Leeds Knights team during the summer, joining fellow former Wild players Alex Mitchell and Harrison Walker, but only played 1 National Division game and 6 Moralee Division games, scoring 7 goals and 1 assist.

Barlow was the Wild's top goalscorer in the Moralee Division last season with 10 goals - and second top points scorer overall in all competitions with 17+20, just 4 short of Joey Coulter, having played 7 games fewer due to injury earlier in the season.

In total in his two previous spells with Widnes, Barlow made 128 appearances, scoring 55+60 with 145 penalty minutes.

Commenting on Barlow's return to the Wild, Widnes Player Coach Tom Jackson said:

"Matty is a massive piece to be returning to the team, during the summer he was initially in my plans for this season but an opportunity to play in the national league enticed him over to Leeds for the start of the season. He is my closest friend living 100m from my doorstep and when things weren't going the way he wanted them to at Leeds I reminded him the door is always open for his return home."

"Matty is a piece that the team has been missing so far this season, he can change the game himself and while doing so can help guide the younger guys on the team. He has had a few weeks off to sort out his personal life and get his new home up and running but will be joining the team on the ice for the foreseeable future."

Bailey Thomson scored the winning goal away at Deeside

(Photo by Keith & Jenny Davies)

Sunday 24th November 2024 – NIHL Moralee Division
Deeside Dragons 4 - Widnes Wild 5

The Widnes Wild NIHL team picked up their first regulation time win of the season with a 4-5 derby day victory away over local rivals Deeside Dragons on Sunday.

Widnes travelled with a very strong squad - quite possibly the strongest line-up they have managed all season following various injuries and other player availability issues - and the difference that this made in their performance was noticeable.

The game was goal-less in the first period and Deeside eventually took the lead with a goal just 1 minute into the second period.

Widnes turned the game on its head with two goals within a minute of each other – from Ross Chalmers and Bailey

Thomson - and led 1-2 at the halfway point in the game. Two more quick fire goals later in the second period – from team captain Andrew Hopkins and Mikey Gilbert further extended the lead but a late strike from Deeside's gifted American Jake Witkowski saw the score standing at 2-4 at the second interval.

Deeside pulled themselves back into contention with a third goal 42 seconds into the third period and the game remained tight until Bailey Thomson scored what would turn out to be the winning goal for Widnes on 55 minutes.

The Dragons removed their netminder for the last minute in the hope of salvaging the game and the addition of an extra attacker helped for a goal with just 30 seconds left. However, the Wild held out as the clock ticked down and managed to secure their first win of the season in regulation time – at the 15th attempt – and the all important 3 points.

Despite the win, Widnes remain bottom of the Moralee Division table with 5 points, 5 behind Sheffield Scimitars and Leeds Knights who both have 10, although they have both played more games.

The Wild are next in action this Sunday 1st December when they take on Whitley Warriors at Planet Ice Widnes, 5.30pm face off.

Damarni James (Photo by Keith & Jenny Davies)

Widnes Wild NIHL player Damarni James has been handed a 2-game suspension by the governing body's Department of Player Safety (DOPS) after having passed the threshold of 10 disciplinary points for the season.

The EIH has a system which involves the accumulation of penalty points for committing offences and receiving penalties prior to, during and after games, which are:

5-minute penalty: 1 point
10-minute misconduct penalty: 2 points
Game misconduct penalty: 4 points
5+ game misconduct penalty: 5 points

James passed the 10 point mark for the season with his 5 minute penalty for fighting in the recent home game against Sheffield Scimitars.

Joe Howie scored his first goal for Widnes against Whitley
(Photo by Keith & Jenny Davies)

Sunday 1st December 2024 – NIHL Moralee Division
Widnes Wild 1 – Whitley Warriors 4

The Widnes Wild NIHL team put in a spirited performance against high flying Whitley Warriors before ultimately losing out 1-4 at Planet Ice Widnes on Sunday.

Having beaten local rivals Deeside Dragons away in North Wales last weekend, the Wild were hoping to build up some sort of run after a disappointing start to the season and this game was pretty close all the way through until Whitley pulled away in the latter stages.

The face off was delayed by 15 minutes because the Whitley team had traffic problems on their way down from the North East and the game didn't start until 5.45pm.

It remained goal-less until Whitley opened the scoring on 15 minutes and a second goal on 18 minutes saw them leading 0-2 at the first period break.

Widnes had their chances in the second period as the Warriors picked up a number of penalties – but they were unable to make the most of their powerplay opportunities and the score remained 0-2 at the second interval.

The Wild pressure did eventually pay off, however, and they finally managed to halve the deficit with their first goal of the game early in the third period, with summer signing Joe Howie scoring his first goal for the club.

Unfortunately, they got into penalty trouble as they pushed forward trying to force an equaliser and conceded a 5 on 3 powerplay goal with 9 minutes left to play. Another powerplay goal 2 minutes later saw Widnes 1-4 down and that was the last scoring action of the game.

The result sees Widnes rooted to the bottom of the Moralee Division table with 5 points from their 16 games to date. They are 5 points behind fellow strugglers Leeds Knights and Sheffield Scimitars, who both have 10 points and have played more games. With Nottingham Lions a rather distant 11 points further ahead than that in 7th place, it looks as if the battle for the 8th place and the final play off spot will be between those three teams.

Widnes have yet to play Nottingham this season - so have four matches against them to look forward to - and they also have two more games against both Sheffield and Leeds to come so there is still plenty to play for as the Moralee Division campaign reaches its half way point.

Will Daley was the Wild's MVP away at Solihull
(Photo by Keith & Jenny Davies)

Saturday 7th December 2024 – NIHL Moralee Division
Solihull Barons 8 - Widnes Wild 2

The Widnes Wild NIHL team's disappointing season continued with an 8-2 defeat to the Solihull Barons away in the West Midlands on Saturday.

The game started well for Widnes with Luke Alston firing them into the lead midway through the first period. Solihull hit back, however, and two goals saw them leading 2-1 at the first period break.

A Mikey Gilbert goal put Widnes back on level terms early in the second period but, once again, they were unable to build on this and three goals for the hosts saw the Barons leading 5-2 at the second interval.

Three more unanswered goals for Solihull in the third period piled on the misery for the travelling Widnes fans and made the final 8-2 scoreline look more one-sided than the Wild performance probably deserved.

The Wild have two more away games this coming weekend - to fellow strugglers Sheffield Scimitars on Saturday 14th December and north west rivals Blackburn Hawks on Sunday 15th.

They are next at home on the last weekend before Christmas when they play Deeside Dragons on Saturday 21st December and Sheffield Scimitars the following day in a mouth-watering double header at Planet Ice Widnes.

Matty Barlow scored two goals in the Wild's win away in Sheffield
(Photo by RDG Digital)

Saturday 14th December 2024 – NIHL Moralee Division: Sheffield Scimitars 1 - Widnes Wild 4

Sunday 15th December 2024 – NIHL Moralee Division: Blackburn Hawks 7 - Widnes Wild 1

The Widnes Wild NIHL team had a mixed weekend, winning 1-4 away at fellow strugglers Sheffield Scimitars on Saturday and then losing 7-1 to Blackburn Hawks on Sunday.

The 9th v 10th game in the Steel City was a "must win" for the Wild if they are to have any chance of lifting themselves away from the bottom of the league table this season and, for once, things went pretty much their way.

Matty Barlow gave the Wild the lead, before a Sheffield equaliser saw the score delicately poised at 1-1 at the first period break. The second period saw goals from Andrew Hopkins and Ross Chalmers fire the Wild to a 1-3 lead by the second break and the win was assured by Barlow's second goal of the game in the third.

Harry Campbell was the Wild's MVP away in Blackburn
(Photo by Nicole Lomax / Hawks Media)

The game away in East Lancashire on Sunday was always going to be the tougher of the two weekend matches for the Wild, and that was exactly how it turned out.

The hosts took a 3-0 lead into the first interval but the Wild had the better of the second period keeping the

Blackburn attack at bay, with Mikey Gilbert firing in a late goal to narrow the deficit.

The Hawks upped their game again in the third period and four unanswered goals saw them cruise to a convincing victory.

After three away games in a row, the Wild are finally back at home this weekend when they play Deeside Dragons on Saturday 21st December (7pm face off) and Sheffield Scimitars the following day (5.30pm) in a mouth-watering double header at Planet Ice Widnes.

*****

The Wild NIHL team will be holding their annual "Air The Bear" Christmas Teddy Toss during Saturday's home game against Deeside Dragons.

Fans are asked to bring a mix of new teddies and dog toys (wrapped in plastic bags to protect them) which will then be thrown onto the ice after the Wild's first goal is scored.

The donations will be gathered up and distributed to Alder Hey Children's Hospital and local animal shelters.

*Wild Head Coach Tom Jackson was in a festive mood at the weekend
(Photo by David Tattum)*

**Saturday 21st December 2024 – NIHL Moralee
Division: Widnes Wild 4 - Deeside Dragons 10**

**Sunday 22nd December 2024 – NIHL Moralee
Division: Widnes Wild 12 - Sheffield Scimitars 4**

The Widnes Wild NIHL team pulled themselves off the
bottom of the Moralee Division table with a sensational
12-4 win over fellow strugglers Sheffield Scimitars at
Planet Ice Widnes on Sunday.

It was a mixed weekend overall for the Wild as they lost
at home to fierce local rivals Deeside Dragons 4-10 but,
considering the season they have had so far, one out of
two ain't bad.

Games against the Dragons are always keen-fought and passionate affairs and Saturday's match was no exception. Spice was added to the occasion by the presence of ex-Wild import Jakub Hajek on the Dragon's bench, along with more former Widnes players in MJ Clancy, Matt Wainwright and Will Harper.

The game actually started well for the Wild and they took the lead with a goal from Tomas Vyrostek after just 4 minutes. Mikey Gilbert fired the Wild 2-0 up two minutes later but then a brace for the Dragons talented American import Jake Witkowski saw the score level at the first period break.

Witkowski fired the Dragons into the lead for the first time on 27 minutes with his hat trick goal and Clancy doubled the advantage for the visitors on 32 minutes.

Owen Rae pulled a goal back for Widnes just 2 minutes later with his first strike of the season but Hajek restored the two-goal cushion 2 minutes after that.

A goal from Wild captain Andrew Hopkins narrowed the deficit to just one on 37th minutes and the score stood at a tantalisingly close 4-5 at the second interval.

Everything went wrong for Widnes in the third period. Deeside scored again just 30 seconds from the restart and four more unanswered goals swept them to a convincing 4-10 victory.

With local bragging rights Deeside-bound down the M56 for the time being, Sunday's game against Sheffield really was a "must win" for the Wild, knowing that a regulation time victory would lift them above the

Bailey Thomson scored 4 goals in the Wild's win over Sheffield on Sunday (Photo by Keith & Jenny Davies)

Scimitars in the league table and off the bottom spot that they had occupied for much of the season.

This game also started well for the Wild, with Bailey Thomson opening the scoring in the 4th minute and from then on, Widnes never looked like losing.

A second goal for Thomson on 14 minutes and then a strike for Mikey Gilbert two minutes later saw them with a 3-1 lead at the first period break and further goals - from Andrew Hopkins, Matty Barlow and Thomson again, for his hat-trick - made it 6-2 at the second interval.

Widnes really ran riot in the third period with goals from Ross Chalmers, Tomas Vyrostek, two more for

Hopkins, a fourth from Thomas and a last minute strike from Damarani James with just 13 seconds left on the clock to round off an impressive victory.

The odd goal here and there from the plucky Sheffield side didn't really matter too much as Widnes were able to celebrate their biggest ever win in the Moralee Division and the first time they have scored double figures since stepping up to the higher league in 2021.

Sunday's win sees the Wild move above Sheffield into 9th place in the 10-team league table – with 11 points to the Scimitars' 10 – and two points behind 8th place Leeds with a game in hand. The Wild now have a break to regroup and, hopefully, build on this achievement when the season restarts in January.

The first weekend of the new year sees them in a double header clash with the Nottingham Lions. They play away in the Lace City on Saturday 4th January – 1pm face off – and then at home the following day at Planet Ice Widnes, 5.30pm start.

The Wild haven't played Nottingham yet this season and they are one of the teams who are on their radar as infinitely catch-able in the race for final league placings. As such, these two games will go a long way to defining the Widnes season as a whole.

*****

Play was interrupted after Tomas Vyrostek's opening goal in the game against Deeside on Saturday – but it was all in a good cause.

It was the Wild's annual "Air The Bear" Christmas Teddy Toss and it has become a tradition that, after the first goal is scored (assuming there is one and it is not a 0-0 draw…) fans throw donations of soft toys onto the ice.

These are then gathered up and distributed to good causes over the festive period

The Teddy Toss was generously supported by the visiting fans from Deeside as well and the toys will be taken to Alder Hey Children's Hospital and local animal shelters.

Tom Jackson and Steve Cunningham deliver Christmas teddies to Alder Hey Children's Hospital (Photo by Widnes Wild IHC)

Wild Deliver Christmas Teddies

Widnes head coach Tom Jackson and General Manager Steve Cunningham made the Wild club's annual visit to deliver teddies to Alder Hey Children's Hospital in Liverpool on Christmas Eve.

The toys had all been donated by kind hearted fans at the "Air The Bear" teddy toss during the recent Widnes Wild v Deeside Dragons local derby game where supporters were invited to throw soft toys out onto the ice at a predetermined moment in the game - and over 150 donations were collected.

Any gifts that weren't suitable to be taken to Alder Hey were separated out and taken to local animal shelters so that homeless pets can have a treat too, meaning that no donation goes to waste!

Widnes Wild NIHL Happy To See Back Of 2024

2024 has not been the most successful of years for the Widnes Wild NIHL team. In fact, critics might point out that it has been their worst calendar year ever in terms of results with just 4 wins out of 17 competitive games at the end of last season and from 22 since the start of the current season

The team only managed 7th place in the Moralee Division table last time out and 7 of their 8 top points scorers for that season moved on to pastures new during the summer, so things were always going to be difficult for new player coach Tom Jackson.

So, with the best will in the world, the Wild are clearly not going to win the Moralee Division league title this season.

They are currently 43 points behind league leaders Billingham Stars with only 45 points left to play for in their remaining 15 games – all which are now against teams that are above them in the table.

They are not going to win the Moralee Cup this season either, having finished bottom of their qualifying group and failed to reach the semi-finals that will be played in January.

However, all is not lost and they still do have some achievable targets to aim for this season.

The first thing would have to be keeping off the bottom of the table – which they finally achieved with a 12-4 win over fellow strugglers Sheffield in their last game of 2024 and which saw them leapfrog the Steel City team and consign the Scimitars to the wooden spoon position.

The next logical objective would be to try and climb into 8th place in the table and qualify for an end of season play off spot. 8th is currently occupied by Leeds Knights who are 2 points ahead of Widnes, having played one game less.

Leeds are a new team to the Moralee Division this season and have also been struggling. They only have four wins to their credit from 20 league games and two of those were against the Wild.

Widnes have two games still to play against Leeds – once home and once away – and, so, could have a realistic chance of catching them – especially if other results go their way as well in the latter stages of the season.

With the season that the Wild have had so far, finishing any higher than 8th would probably be viewed as an added bonus.

Nottingham Lions are having a good season this time around and currently occupy 7th position - with a 9 point lead over Leeds and 13 points over Widnes.

Interestingly enough, with the way that the fixture list has panned out this season, Widnes haven't played Nottingham yet and have 4 games against them – 2 home and 2 away – still to come.

It just so turns out that the first weekend of the new year sees Widnes in a double header clash with the Lions.

They play away in the Lace City on Saturday 4th January –
1pm face off – and then at home the following day at
Planet Ice Widnes, 5.30pm start. The way things stand at
the moment, these two games will go a long way to
defining the Widnes season as a whole.

Saturday 4ᵗʰ January 2025
NIHL Moralee Division
Nottingham Lions P
Widnes Wild P

Sunday 5ᵗʰ January 2025
NIHL Moralee Division
Widnes Wild P
Nottingham Lions P

Joe Howie
(Photo by Keith & Jenny Davies)

Despite being a winter sport, ice hockey fell victim to the weather this weekend and the Widnes Wild NIHL team found themselves without a game.

They had been due to play a juicy double header against Nottingham Lions - away in the Lace City on Saturday and then at home at Planet Ice Widnes on Sunday - in a pair of games where victories might have seen them pull further away from the bottom of the Moralee Division table, following their timely win over Sheffield Scimitars in the last game of 2024.

Unfortunately, the away game on Saturday was called off due to issues in the Nottingham camp and then with heavy snowfall across the country over Saturday night, and an amber weather warning from the Met Office remaining in place throughout Sunday, it was deemed unwise for the Lions to undertake the journey across the Pennines and, indeed, a number of games in NIHL North were postponed on safety grounds.

It is hoped that alternative dates can be found for these two games later in the season – especially as Nottingham are one of the teams that Widnes have a chance of overtaking in the league table, if results go their way.

However, with a number of teams now needing to re-arrange unplayed games, this will have a knock-on effect across the league. Also, with ice time being difficult to secure at Nottingham's home rink due to the number of other teams that also play there, it could become a scheduling nightmare for the sport's governing body, England Ice Hockey.

Because of a quirk in the fixture list, Widnes haven't played Nottingham yet this season, meaning that 4 of their remaining 15 league games will be against the Lions, twice home and twice away. Former Lions player Joe Howie joined the Wild in the summer and the weekend postponements mean that he will have to wait a little longer to come up against his former team-mates.

Weather permitting, Widnes will be back in action this weekend with a visit on Saturday 11th January to Leeds Knights – who are just above them in the league table, occupying the last play off spot - and then at home to Solihull Barons on Sunday at Planet Ice Widnes.

Andrew Hopkins scored 3 goals over the weekend
(Photo by Keith & Jenny Davies)

Saturday 11th January 2025 – NIHL Moralee Division
Leeds Knights 7 – Widnes Wild 2

Sunday 12th January 2025 – NIHL Moralee Division
Widnes Wild 5 – Solihull Barons 7

The Widnes Wild NIHL team got 2025 off to a losing start with a 7-2 defeats away to Leeds Knights on Saturday and then a narrow 5-7 loss at home to Solihull Barons at Planet Ice Widnes on Sunday

A win on Saturday would have seen Widnes overtake Leeds in the Moralee Division table and move up to the dizzy heights of 8th place and a play off spot. But it was not to be and goals from Owen Rae and Andrew Hopkins were not enough to stave off a 7-2 defeat.

Unfortunately, the loss – the Wild's third of the season at the hands of the Moralee Division's newest team – was instead compounded by a surprise win for fellow strugglers Sheffield Scimitars, who beat Hull Jets on penalty shots on Saturday. That win lifted Sheffield back above Widnes in the table, leaving them rock bottom in 10th position.

The Wild put up a much better fight against the visiting Barons on Sunday and, had they had the rub of the green, they might well have got something out of the game.

The score was 3-3 at the end of the closely contested first period, with the Widnes goals coming from Tomas Vyrostek, Matty Barlow and a Penalty Shot from team captain Andrew Hopkins

Hopkins and Barlow both scored again in the second period but three goals for Solihull – who had been boosted by the signing of talented player Zach Yokoyama - took a 5-6 lead into the second interval. Despite numerous chances at both ends, the only goal of the third period fell to Solihull and they were able to celebrate a 5-7 victory.

Despite the defeat, Harry Campbell was impressive in the Widnes goal, keeping out 49 of the 56 shots that he faced - and Will Daley received the MVP (Most Valuable Player) Award for the Wild.

The Widnes Wild NIHL team are next in action this Saturday 18th January when they travel away to face the Nottingham Lions, 1pm face off. They are next at home the week after when they entertain high-flying north-west rivals Blackburn Hawks on Saturday 25th January at Planet Ice Widnes, 7pm face off.

Dani Haid in Solihull colours (Photo by Keith & Jenny Davies)

Saturday 18th January 2025 – NIHL Moralee Division
Nottingham Lions 3 – Widnes Wild 5

The Widnes Wild NIHL team gave their play off hopes a boost with a highly important 3-5 win away to Nottingham Lions on Saturday.

The first period played out goal-less and it remained goal-less until Nottingham finally broke the deadlock with the opening goal in the 28th minute.

4 minutes later, the score was 2-0 to the Lions and it looked as if the Wild could be in trouble. However, they rallied from this and a goal late in the period from Bailey Thomson kept Widnes in contention, and the score stood at 2-1 at the second interval.

Nottingham edged further ahead on 45 minutes but a Wild goal from Ben McLellan 40 seconds later reduced the deficit back to just one

Widnes were on a roll by now and Luke Alston fired in the equalising goal on 49 minutes but received a heavy challenge for his trouble. McLellan piled in to stick up for his team-mate and was subsequently banished from the game for a check to the head on the wrongdoer.

The Wild dug deep and managed to weather the ensuing 5 minute powerplay and Dani Haid fired them into the lead for the first time in the game with a goal on 56 minutes.

Nottingham withdrew their netminder in favour of an extra attacker in the hope of salvaging something from the game but Bailey Thomson scored an Empty Net Goal with 56 seconds left on the clock to seal the win for Widnes.

With Sheffield Scimitars not playing at the weekend, Saturday's win sees the Wild leapfrog them off the bottom of the Moralee Division table into 9th place, three points behind Leeds Knights whom occupy the final play off spot.

The Widnes Wild NIHL team are next in action on Saturday 25th January when they entertain high-flying north-west rivals Blackburn Hawks at Planet Ice Widnes, 7pm face off.

Flynn Massie (Photo by Steve Cunningham)

Wild NIHL Player News

The Wild team away at Nottingham was boosted by the return of two former players after Dani Haid and Flynne Massie rejoined the club for the remainder of the season.

German national Haid played 86 games for Widnes between 2019 and 2023 and was part of the Wild team that won the North21 cup, the Division 1 National Championship and the 2021/22 Moralee Cup, scoring 40 goals, 23 assists and picking up just 15 penalty minutes. He has spent the last season and a half playing for Solihull Barons, scoring 10+7 in 47 games.

Scottish junior international Massie played 14 games for the Wild last season as part of a two way deal with SNL team North Ayrshire Wild, scoring two goals and 4 assists. He has spent this season in Frankfurt in Germany.

Will Daley (Photo by Keith & Jenny Davies)

The Wild team have announced that defenceman Will Daley has left the club. 16 year old Daley joined Widnes as his first senior NIHL club after playing junior hockey with Whitley Bay, Billingham and Solway and has played 21 games for Widnes this season.

Wild Head Coach, Tom Jackson said of Daley's departure: "Will called me last week and I spoke with him and his dad, Chris at length about Will's situation with the club and unfortunately as a family, they have chosen to request his release."

"I would like to take this opportunity to wish Will and his family all the best for the future. Will came in from day one and earned his spot on the team as one of the mainstays this season, his competitiveness and ability will certainly be missed. He was a young kid who asked the right questions, rarely made mistakes and was a pleasure to coach. If he continues playing like he can, he will be an asset on any team he plays for."

"Despite the short time he spent at Widnes he wanted to leave the right way and asked to play one more time with the guys (last weekend - against Solihull) and say his goodbyes to the team. For me this shows great character and the door for his return will remain open while I'm in this role."

Talking about leaving the Wild, Daley said: "I would like to thank everyone involved at the club and the fans for the opportunity that has been given to me this season. I've really loved my time at Widnes and would like to thank TJ and the coaching staff for having me as part of the team, I have made friends for life within the squad. Due to travel and college commitments, I can't continue with the club unfortunately."

Following his departure from Widnes, Daley was immediately snapped up by fellow Moralee Division team Whitley Warriors.

Damarni James missed the game at Nottingham after having been handed a 6-game suspension by the governing body's Department of Player Safety (DOPS).

He picked up a 5 plus game ban penalty in the match away at Leeds for an illegal check to the head which resulted in a 3-game suspension and has also been given an extra 3 games for reaching the threshold of 15 disciplinary points for the season.

Damarni James (Photo by Keith & Jenny Davies)

The EIH(A) has a system which involves the accumulation of disciplinary points for committing offences and receiving penalties prior to, during and after games. The disciplinary points are applied as follows:

5-minute penalty: 1 point
10-minute misconduct penalty: 2 points
Game misconduct penalty: 4 points
5+ game misconduct penalty: 5 points

When a player or team has accrued a certain number of disciplinary points – according to a fixed scale – sanctions such as suspensions or fines can be imposed.

Bez Hughes scored his first Wild goal of the season against Blackburn
(Photo by Keith & Jenny Davies)

Saturday 25th January 2025 – NIHL Moralee Division
Widnes Wild 2 – Blackburn Hawks 6

The Widnes Wild NIHL team put in a battling performance against north west rivals Blackburn Hawks but ultimately lost out 2-6 at Planet Ice Widnes on Saturday.

Games between Widnes and Blackburn are always keenly contested affairs but, with the Wild struggling to draw clear of the cellar regions of the Moralee Division league table and second place Blackburn still in with an outside chance of the league title, this was always going to be a bit of a tough test.

Despite missing a few key players, Widnes gave as good as they got and it was a very close 0-1 at the end of the first period. The score was 0-4 at the end of the second -

due mainly to a hat-trick from former Wild player Adam Barnes - and he added his fourth goal in the third period to bring the Hawks' tally to 6 for the night.

A short-handed goal from Dani Haid and a strike from Bez Hughes – his first goal of the season - gave the final score a more respectable look and the Wild need not be too disheartened with their overall performance against one of the top teams in the division.

Widnes's former Hawks player Ben McLellan was missing from the game after he was handed a 3-game suspension by the sport's governing body for a check to the head in the away game at Nottingham the week before. Damarni James – another ex- Hawk - is also suspended with a 6-game ban for having reached the threshold of 15 disciplinary points after being thrown out of the away game against Leeds.

With fellow strugglers Sheffield losing 9-1 at Billingham over the weekend and Leeds losing 6-3 at Blackburn, Widnes remain in 9th place in the Moralee Division table, within sniffing distance of a play off spot with 11 regular season games left to play.

Borderline strugglers Nottingham Lions shocked Deeside with a 10-5 win on Sunday night that draws them clear in 7th place from the melee below them with a 12 point cushion

The Wild are next in action this Saturday 1st February when they take on Hull Jets at Planet Ice Widnes, 7pm face off.

Jonathan Williamson and Mikey Gilbert in action away at Blackburn
(Photo by Steve Pollitt)

Saturday 8th February 2025 – NIHL Moralee Division
Blackburn Hawks 4 – Widnes Wild 2

Sunday 9th February 2025 – NIHL Moralee Division
Widnes Wild 1 – Billingham Stars 3

The Widnes Wild NIHL team had a tough weekend, taking on the top two teams in the league, losing 8-2 away to Blackburn Hawks on Saturday and 1-3 at home to Billingham Stars at Planet Ice Widnes on Sunday.

Blackburn never really looked like losing on Saturday and went ahead with goals from former Wild player Adam Barnes and promising teenager Daragh Spawforth. A goal from Andrew Hopkins on 18 minutes halved the deficit for Widnes and the score stood at 2-1 at the first period break.

The Hawks scored 4 unanswered goals in the second period to put the game well beyond Widnes' reach and added two more in the third. A late strike from Matty Barlow with three minutes left on the clock gave the travelling fans something to cheer about but the game finished in a convincing 8-2 win for Blackburn.

While the result on Saturday may have been somewhat predictable, the game on Sunday certainly wasn't as the Wild put in a barnstorming performance against the league leaders.

Widnes played out of their skins – clearly rattling the Billingham Stars - and for much of the game, it was hard to tell that there were 8 league places - and 58 points - between the two teams.

After a tense opening, Billingham eventually took the lead and the score remained at a very tight 0-1 at the first period break.

The Widnes attacking efforts were finally rewarded on 25 minutes when captain Andrew Hopkins fired in a rebound off a Matty Barlow shot to equalise with a powerplay goal and despite numerous chances at both ends, the teams remained locked at 1-1 after two periods.

This was the closest that the Wild had been against any of the top teams all season and it really looked as if an upset might be on the cards as the score remained 1-1 heading into the final 10 minutes.

The tension around the Planet Ice rink was electrifying as the extremely vocal Widnes support urged their team on. Unfortunately, it was not to be and two late goals secured the win for the Stars.

Despite the disappointing end result, there was nothing to fault about the Wild performance. Paul Maudsley played an absolute blinder in goal, having been given his first start in the Widnes net after a number of back-up stints, and went on to be deservedly awarded the MVP for the Wild.

Talking afterwards about the two weekend games, Mikey Gilbert said:

"We were going into an extremely tough weekend against the top 2 teams as major underdogs and people would have been expecting hammerings against vastly more experienced teams with big name players playing for them. And then even moreso when we didn't have our starting goalie."

"However as a team we stuck together and beared down. Played simple, worked hard and made sure we battled for each other."

"Both games were really competitive end to end for the most part of both of them. The Sunday game sticking out for us even more keeping the top of the league team to 1-1 with 10 mins left to only concede when we were pushing even more to get the go ahead goal."

"We created lots of offence in both games and really worked as a solid Unit in defence limiting chances as much as possible and keeping opposition to lower scoring areas. And Maudsley playing really well on Sunday too."

With bottom club Sheffield losing 11-4 away to Whitley and Leeds Knights losing twice - to Whitley and Hull – all remains the same at the bottom of the Moralee Division table. Widnes stay in 9th place out of 10 teams, two points ahead of the Scimitars with games in hand - which should keep them clear of the wooden spoon - and 6 points behind Leeds, who currently occupy the last play off spot.

The Wild have three away games now in a row – starting with a trip to face the Solihull Barons on Sunday 16th February, and back to back road games against Deeside Dragons and Nottingham Lions the week after. They are next at home on Sunday 2nd March when they take on Leeds Knights at Planet Ice Widnes, 5.30pm face off.

Netminder Paul Maudsley was the Wild MVP against Billingham (Photo by David Tattum)

Dani Haid scored against his old club away at Solihull
(Photo by David Tattum)

Sunday 16th February 2025 – NIHL Moralee Division
Solihull Barons 12 Widnes Wild 5

The Widnes Wild NIHL team suffered a 12 –5 defeat away to Solihull Barons on Sunday.

Solihull opened the scoring on 3 minutes and went 2-0 up on 14 minutes. Dani Haid pulled a goal back for Widnes against his former club on 19 minutes and the score stood at 2-1 at the first break.

4 goals early on in the second period saw Solihull begin to pull away but Nathan Pollard - making his Wild debut - scored on 38 minutes to stem the flow. However a further Solihull goal just 10 seconds later saw the Barons leading 7-2 after two periods.

The hosts further extended their lead 57 seconds into the third period but Damarni James pulled a goal back for Widnes on 43 minutes. Two more Solihull goals were followed by a Mikey Gilbert strike, leaving the score at 10-4 with 10 minutes left to play.

Yet two more goals brought the Barons' tally to a round dozen for the night and a strike for Kai Hathaway rounded off the Wild scoring.

The Wild have two more away games in a row - against local rivals Deeside Dragons this Saturday 22nd February and away to Nottingham Lions on Sunday. They are next at home on Sunday 2nd March when they take on Leeds Knights at Planet Ice Widnes, 5.30pm face off.

Kai Hathaway was on target for Widnes in Solihull
(Photo by Keith & Jenny Davies)

Flynn Massie scored in both games at the weekend
(Photo by David Tattum)

Saturday 22nd February 2025 – NIHL Moralee Division
Deeside Dragons 9 - Widnes Wild 8

Sunday 23rd February 2025 – NIHL Moralee Division
Nottingham Lions 6 - Widnes Wild 2

The Widnes Wild NIHL team had a disappointing weekend on the road, narrowly losing out 9-8 to north-west rivals Deeside Dragons on Saturday and then slumping to a 6-2 defeat to Nottingham Lions on Sunday.

Games between Widnes and Deeside are always close fought and passionate affairs and Saturday's was up among the best of them as it turned out to be a 17-goal thriller.

Deeside opened the scoring after just 22 seconds with a goal from their talented American forward Jake Witkowski but Widnes hit back just 60 seconds later with an equaliser from Luke Alston.

Two goals for Deeside within 8 seconds of each other fired them into a 3-1 lead but strikes from Damarni James and then Dani Haid put Widnes back on level terms. A second goal from Witkowski edged the Dragons back in front on 15 minutes and the score remained 4-3 at the first period break.

Deeside scored again 21 seconds into the second period and then a powerplay goal saw them go 6-3 up. Ben McLellan pulled a goal back for Widnes at the half way mark of the game but a hat-trick goal for Witkowski with just 52 seconds left on the clock saw the Dragons leading 7-4 at the second interval.

Matty Barlow pulled a goal back for Widnes 90 seconds into the third period but this was countered by another Deeside strike. Wild captain Andrew Hopkins scored for Widnes on 48 minutes and, on 51 minutes Flynn Massie fired the puck home to narrow the deficit to just 1 goal.

A Dragons counter-strike just 25 sends after that restored the two-goal cushion but Matty Barlow gave the vocal travelling fans some hope as he fired in his second goal of the game with just over two minutes left to play.

Unfortunately, the Wild were not able to build any further on this and the game finished in a terribly close 9-8 win for the Dragons.

On paper, the game at Nottingham on Sunday might have seemed like the easier of the two weekend fixtures but this turned out not to be the case and the Lions were on top of things right from the start.

Nottingham led 2-0 after the first period and the score was 5-1 at the second break, with the Widnes goal coming from Flynn Massie – his second in two games.

The Lions scored again in the third period, putting the match well out of the Wild's reach but Dani Haid fired in a goal with 3 minutes left to play to give the final score a slightly more respectable look.

The weekend results leave Widnes stuck in 9th place in the Moralee Division table, two points clear of bottom team Sheffield and 6 points behind Leeds, who occupy the final play off position in 8th.

Three of the Wild's final 5 games of the regular season are at home against "bottom half" teams and if they were to win all of those, they could feasible - and depending on results elsewhere - still qualify for the play offs.

The Wild are at home this Sunday 2nd March when they take on Leeds Knights at Planet Ice Widnes, 5.30pm face off.

Matty Barlow scored the OT winner for Widnes and was named MVP
(Photo by David Tattum)

Sunday 2nd March 2025 – NIHL Moralee Division
Widnes Wild 5 – Leeds Knights 4 (OT)

The Widnes Wild NIHL team put an end to their 7-game losing streak with a hard fought and well deserved 5-4 overtime win against Leeds Knights at Planet Ice Widnes on Sunday.

As the final score suggests, this was a very close game between teams who were 8th and 9th in the league table and there was very little to choose between the two teams all the way through.

Leeds took the lead on 5 minutes but Luke Alston equalised for the Wild on 13 minutes and the score remained 1-1 at the first period break.

The second period was just as close and Widnes took the lead with a back door tap in from captain Andrew Hopkins on 31 minutes. However, Leeds hit back 5 minutes later and the match was all tied at a very finely balanced 2-2 at the second interval.

The third period was goal-less for the first 10 minutes but Bez Hughes fired in to edge the Wild ahead again at 50.20. Leeds equalised two minutes later and got their noses back in front with another goal on 57 minutes to take a 3-4 lead. Two minutes after that, with just 74 seconds left on the clock, Mikey Gilbert scored to put the Wild back on level terms and send the game into a nail-biting period of sudden death over time.

Matty Barlow popped up as the hero of the piece as he fired in the golden goal winner, giving the Wild their first victory since mid-January. It was their second overtime win of the season - and their 6th win overall.

Unfortunately, as far as the league table is concerned, an overtime win only yields two league points for the winners instead of the 3 for a regular time win, and it also gives the losing team one point for having been level at the end of 60 minutes.

This means that Leeds' advantage is now down to 5 points from 6 in the race for 8th spot, with both teams having 4 games left to play. Widnes have two games coming up against 7th place Nottingham Lions but also a tricky weekend on the road with trips to Hull and Whitley.

They are next in action this Saturday 8th March when they play the first of those crunch ties at home to Nottingham at Planet Ice Widnes, 7pm face off.

*Andrew Hopkins scored a hat-trick for the Wild against Nottingham
(Photo by Keith & Jenny Davies)*

Saturday 8th March 2025 – NIHL Moralee Division
Widnes Wild 8 – Nottingham Lions 4

The Widnes Wild NIHL team gave their end of season play off hopes a huge boost with an 8-4 win over Nottingham Lions at Planet Ice Widnes on Saturday.

The result came hot on the heels of last week's win over fellow strugglers Leeds Knights and is the first time all season that the Wild have managed back to back victories.

The Wild took a very narrow lead into the first break with the only goal of the period from

Kai Hathaway – and netminder Harry Campbell performed heroics in the Widnes goal to keep the Lions' attack at bay.

Wild captain Andrew Hopkins doubled the lead for Widnes early in the second period but 2 quick-fire goals from Nottingham drew the Lions level.

Dani Haid edged Widnes back into the lead with a powerplay goal but Nottingham equalised once again. However the Widnes players didn't give up and their pressure was rewarded with a goal from Matty Barlow and a short handed strike from Hopkins to finish the period with a 5-3 lead.

Three more goals in the third period for Widnes – a hat-trick strike from Hopkins, a second goal for Barlow and an empty net goal from Luke Alston – and a single response from Nottingham – saw the Wild cruise to an important victory in their late season push for the play offs

Leeds Knights currently occupy the coveted 8th spot and last play off place but, with them losing away to Deeside on Sunday, their advantage over the Wild is now down to just 2 points.

Both teams have three games to play and Leeds are probably still in the driving seat as two of theirs are at home, while Widnes have two away. Rather intriguingly, both teams play Nottingham Lions at home on the last weekend of the regular season – Widnes on the Saturday and Leeds on the Sunday – and, depending on how other results go in the meantime, those two games could well decide who gets the last play off place.

Widnes now have a tricky weekend on the road with trips to Hull this Saturday 15th March and Whitley on Sunday.

They are then back at home for their final game of the regular season at home to Nottingham on Saturday 22nd March at Planet Ice Widnes, 7pm face off.

*Netminder Harry Campbell was the Wild MVP away at Whitley
(Photo by Charlie Mood)*

Saturday 15th March 2025 – NIHL Moralee Division Whitley Warriors 3 - Widnes Wild 1

Sunday 16th March 2025 – NIHL Moralee Division Hull Jets 7 - Widnes Wild 5

The Widnes Wild NIHL team put in two battling performances on the road at the weekend, narrowly losing out 3-1 away to Whitley Bay on Saturday and 7-5 at Hull on Sunday.

The game on Saturday in the north east was especially close and remained goal-less at the first period break. Whitley took a single goal lead into the second interval and two more goals in the third period game handed them the victory, although a consolation strike from Flynn Massie kept the Wild in contention right up to the final buzzer.

Widnes got off to a slow start in the game on Humberside on Sunday. The Jets raced to a 4 goal lead before Mikey Gilbert pulled one back for the Wild - but former Widnes player Adam Jasecko fired in to give the hosts a 5-1 lead at the first interval.

The second period was closer and two goals from Matty Barlow and one from Andrew Hopkins saw the score standing at 7-4 with one period left to play. The only goal of the third period fell to the Wild's Luke Alston but Widnes were unable to build any further on this and the game ended up at 7-5 to Hull.

Despite the two weekend defeats, Widnes still have an outside chance of reaching the end of season play offs. They are currently 2 points behind Leeds Knights – who occupy the coveted 8th spot in the league table but they absolutely have to win their last game of the season – at home to Nottingham Lions on Saturday – for there to be any hope of overtaking them.

Leeds have two games left – away at Sheffield on Saturday and at home to Nottingham on Sunday - and just a single point from either of those games would mean that they could not be caught and would take the final play off spot.

The Widnes Wild NIHL team play their last game of the regular season this Saturday 22nd March when they take on Nottingham Lions at Planet Ice Widnes, 7pm face off.

Bez Hughes was the Wild's MVP in their last game of the season - at home to Nottingham. (Photo by Keith & Jenny Davies)

Saturday 22nd March 2025 – NIHL Moralee Division
Widnes Wild 7 - Nottingham Lions 5

The Widnes Wild NIHL team finished the season on a winning note with a thrilling 7-5 victory over Nottingham Lions at Planet Ice Widnes on Saturday.

Nottingham took an early lead just 9 seconds into the game but goals from Mikey Gilbert and Andrew Hopkins saw Widnes leading 2-1 at the first period break.

The second period was another belter with three goals coming for each side. Matty Barlow, Dani Haid and Luke Alston were all on target for the Wild ensuring that Widnes went into the second interval with a slender 5-4 lead.

The third period was just as closely fought and Nottingham made quite a fight of it but two goals from Barlow in the third period – rounding off a well-deserved hat-trick - settled matters and the Wild were able to celebrate their third home win in a row

With Leeds Knights losing away at Sheffield, the three league points from the win temporarily lifted Widnes up into 8th place in the Moralee Division table, occupying the final play off spot. However, Leeds were due to play Nottingham on the Sunday and if they won that game, they would leapfrog back above the Wild in the final standings.

As it turned out, Nottingham looked as if they would be doing the Wild a big favour in Leeds as they raced to a 0-3 lead in the game on Sunday. The Knights fought back, however, tying the match 3-3 at the end of regulation time, and then went on to win 4-3 in overtime. The OTW gave them 2 points and means that they finish just 1 point ahead of the Wild in the final Moralee Division table, securing the 8th and final play off spot.

The quarter final pairings for the Play Offs are based on final league positions with 1st v 8th, 2nd v 7th and so on. This means that the line up for the quarter finals is Billingham Stars v Leeds Knights, Blackburn Hawks v Nottingham Lions, Solihull Barons v Whitley Warriors and Deeside Dragons v Hull Jets.

The ties will be played over two legs, home and away, this Saturday 29th and Sunday 30th March, with the winning teams progressing to two-legged semi finals the weekend after.

The Play Off finals for all four regional NIHL Divisions will take place as part of the Steel City Showdown weekend in Sheffield on Saturday 12th April.

Andy Hopkins receives the Player Of The Year award from Danny Cliffe of DMH Tyres (left) and Wild Head Coach Tom Jackson (Photo by Steve Cunningham)

13th June: Wild Presentation Night

The Widnes Wild NIHL team held their end of season Presentation Night at The Venue venue in Widnes Town centre on Friday 13th June.

As ever, it was a fun-filled relaxed evening where players, team staff, match volunteers and fans could get together to look back over the past season. There was dancing, a buffet and shirt sponsors were able to collect their "Own and Loan" playing shirts.

A new innovation for this season was for local companies and individuals to sponsor the various awards.

The various awards were presented as follows:

- Player Of The Year (sponsored by DMH Tyres) – Andrew Hopkins
- Players' Player Of The Year (sponsored by On The Go mechanics) – Andrew Hopkins
- Coaches' Player Of The Year (sponsored by the Jackson family) – Ben McLellan
- GM's Player Of The Year (sponsored by Shots By Ste) – Luke Alston
- Defensive Player Of The Year (sponsored by Puck Yeah!) – Jonathan Williamson
- Forward Of The Year (sponsored by Puck Yeah!) – Mikey Gilbert
- Fans' Defensive Player Of The Year (sponsored by Puck Yeah!) – Harry Campbell
- Fans' Forward Of The Year (sponsored by Widnes Wild Ones) – Flynn Massie
- Ken Armstrong Award (sponsored by DMH Tyres) – Bez Hughes

The evening also saw long service awards for three players who had reached particular milestones during the past season.

Mikey Gilbert and Bez Hughes were both fêted for having passed 200 games for the Wild while Jonathan Williamson passed 100 games for Widnes this season.

WNIHL Division 2 North – Season 2024/25

Final Table	GP	W	D	L	GF	GA	GD	Pts
Widnes Wild Women	12	7	4	1	56	36	20	18
Telford Wrekin Raiders	12	7	2	3	72	31	41	16
Sheffield Shadows	12	8	0	4	55	29	26	16
Leeds Roses	12	6	3	3	75	32	43	15
Whitley Bay Beacons	12	5	1	6	50	50	0	11
Kingston Diamonds	12	3	2	7	33	74	-41	8
Caledonia Bees	12	0	0	12	28	117	-89	0

Top Points Scorers

Player	Team	GP	G	A	Pts	PIM
C.J. Harrison	Leeds Roses	11	19	9	28	2
Jasmin Daniel	Leeds Roses	10	16	9	25	0
Tiffany-Jayne Miller	Telford Raiders	11	11	14	25	6
Leen de Decker	Widnes Wild	10	15	6	21	0
Heather Metcalf	Telford Raiders	12	8	13	21	8
Maggie Whitmore	Telford Raiders	11	14	6	20	8
Isabella Oswin	Kingston D'monds	9	12	6	18	4
Chloe Carter	Sheffield Shadows	10	12	4	16	12
Athene Idiabor-Moses	Sheffield Shadows	11	5	10	15	4
Charlotte Cramp	Widnes Wild	10	8	6	14	0

Top Netminders

Netminder	Team	GPI	Mins	SA	GA	GAA	SV%	SO
Kirsty Robson	SHE	11	409	200	15	2.2	92.50%	2
Teagan Hyatt	TEL	7	420	241	16	2.29	93.40%	1
Emily Johnson	KIN	8	403	292	21	3.13	92.80%	0
Barthe McCormick	LEE	4	227	151	11	2.92	92.70%	0
Shannon Schneider	SHE	2	40	13	1	1.5	92.30%	1
Dawn Dickinson	KIN	1	49	35	3	3.74	91.40%	0
Alice Somerford	TEL/LEE	5	300	158	14	2.8	91.10%	1
Keira Daniel	LEE	2	120	77	7	3.5	90.90%	0
Steph Drinkwater	WID	11	647	418	39	3.62	90.70%	1
Ruth Palmer	WHI	12	720	345	50	4.17	85.50%	0

Widnes Wild Women Player Statistics – 2024/25
WNIHL Division 2 North

Player	GP	G	A	Pts	PIM
Leen de Decker	10	15	6	21	0
Charlotte Cramp	10	9	6	15	0
Lise Gillen	8	8	1	12	4
Amanda Armstrong	7	5	5	10	0
Jennifer Hickey	11	2	6	8	2
Phoebe Patient	7	4	2	6	2
Ellen Tyrer	7	2	4	6	2
Karyn Cooper	11	0	6	6	2
Ruth Leopold	12	4	1	5	2
Jemma Brown	11	4	1	5	4
Victoria Connelly	7	1	4	5	0
Rachael Pearce	12	0	5	5	8
Abigail Aldred	7	2	2	4	0
Charlotte McAdam	8	1	2	3	0
Catherine Fell	8	0	3	3	8
Katie Fairclough	8	1	1	2	31
Eleanor Johnson	10	0	2	2	2
Jennifer Greenwood	8	0	1	1	2
Lucy Kirkham	6	0	1	1	2
Savannah Sumner	3	0	1	1	2
Suzie Miller	10	0	0	0	2
Katie Adshead	10	0	0	0	4
Elizabeth Loss	9	0	0	0	2
Vanessa Crickmore-Clarke	8	0	0	0	2
Laura Moran	8	0	0	0	6
Sophie Hill	6	0	0	0	0
Niamh Horsfield	2	0	0	0	0
Nicole Rainey	1	0	0	0	0
Stephanie Drinkwater	11	0	0	0	0
Charlotte Jackson	1	0	0	0	0

Netminder	GPI	Min	SA	GA	GAA	Save %	SO
Stephanie Drinkwater	11	646	421	32	2.97	92.40	1
Charlotte Jackson	1	60	38	4	4.00	89.47	0
Totals	12	706	459	36	3.06	92.16	1

Please note that the goals and assists for the away game at Caledonia were taken from Wild Women's team coach Paddy Horner's notes and NOT from the official gamesheet, so our player stats for the season may not tally with other official figures.

Widnes Wild Women Player Statistics – 2024/25
WNIHL Division 2 North Cup

Player	GP	G	A	Pts	PIM
Katie Fairclough	3	4	1	5	0
Leen de Decker	4	1	4	5	2
Rachael Pearce	4	2	2	4	4
Catherine Fell	4	1	2	3	2
Karyn Cooper	4	2	0	2	0
Amanda Armstrong	2	1	1	2	0
Jemma Brown	2	1	1	2	0
Cath Thornton	3	1	0	1	0
Suzie Miller	4	0	0	0	0
Jennifer Hickey	4	0	0	0	0
Jennifer Greenwood	4	0	0	0	0
Eleanor Johnson	4	0	0	0	0
Katie Adshead	3	0	0	0	0
Charlotte McAdam	3	0	0	0	0
Elizabeth Loss	2	0	0	0	0
Ruth Leopold	2	0	0	0	0
Niamh Horsfield	2	0	0	0	0
Sophie Hill	2	0	0	0	0
Ellen Tyrer	1	0	0	0	0
Lucy Kirkham	1	0	0	0	0
Charlotte Cramp	1	0	0	0	0
Vanessa Crickmore-Clarke	1	0	0	0	0
Stephanie Drinkwater	3	0	0	0	0
Charlotte Jackson	1	0	0	0	0

Netminder	GPI	Min	SA	GA	GAA	Save %	SO
Stephanie Drinkwater	3	161.3	157	22	8.18	85.99	0
Charlotte Jackson	1	60	59	13	13.00	77.97	0
Totals	4	221.3	216	35	9.49	83.80	0

Widnes Wild Women Player Statistics – 2024/25
WNIHL D2N Play Offs

Player	GP	G	A	Pts	PIM
Leen de Decker	1	1	0	1	0
Lise Gillen	1	0	1	1	0
Eleanor Johnson	1	0	1	1	0
Charlotte Cramp	1	0	0	0	0
Jennifer Hickey	1	0	0	0	0
Phoebe Patient	1	0	0	0	0
Karyn Cooper	1	0	0	0	0
Ruth Leopold	1	0	0	0	2
Jemma Brown	1	0	0	0	0
Victoria Connelly	1	0	0	0	0
Rachael Pearce	1	0	0	0	0
Abigail Aldred	1	0	0	0	2
Charlotte McAdam	1	0	0	0	0
Catherine Fell	1	0	0	0	0
Suzie Miller	1	0	0	0	0
Katie Adshead	1	0	0	0	0
Elizabeth Loss	1	0	0	0	0
Vanessa Crickmore-Clarke	1	0	0	0	0
Laura Moran	1	0	0	0	2
Stephanie Drinkwater	1	0	0	0	0

Netminder	GPI	Min	SA	GA	GAA	Save %	SO
Stephanie Drinkwater	1	60	50	8	8.00	84.00	0

Widnes Wild Women Player Statistics – 2024/25
All Matches (includes League, Cup & Play Offs

Player	GP	G	A	Pts	PIM
Leen de Decker	15	17	10	27	2
Charlotte Cramp	12	9	6	15	0
Lise Gillen	9	8	2	13	4
Amanda Armstrong	9	6	6	12	0
Rachael Pearce	17	2	7	9	12
Jennifer Hickey	16	2	6	8	2
Karyn Cooper	16	2	6	8	2
Jemma Brown	14	5	2	7	4
Katherine Fairclough	11	5	2	7	31
Catherine Fell	13	1	5	6	10
Phoebe Patient	8	4	2	6	2
Ellen Tyrer	8	2	4	6	2
Ruth Leopold	15	4	1	5	4
Victoria Connelly	8	1	4	5	0
Abigail Aldred	8	2	2	4	2
Eleanor Johnson	15	0	3	3	2
Charlotte McAdam	12	1	2	3	0
Jennifer Greenwood	12	0	1	1	2
Lucy Kirkham	7	0	1	1	2
Savannah Sumner	3	0	1	1	2
Cath Thornton	3	1	0	1	0
Suzanne Miller	15	0	0	0	2
Stephanie Drinkwater	15	0	0	0	0
Katie Adshead	14	0	0	0	4
Elizabeth Loss	12	0	0	0	2
Vanessa Crickmore-Clarke	10	0	0	0	2
Laura Moran	9	0	0	0	8
Sophie Hill	8	0	0	0	0
Niamh Horsfield	4	0	0	0	0
Charlotte Jackson	2	0	0	0	0
Nicole Rainey	1	0	0	0	0

Netminder	Comp	GPI	Mins	SA	GA	GAA	Save %	SO
Stephanie Drinkwater	League	11	646.05	421	32	2.97	92.40	1
	Cup	3	161.19	157	22	8.18	85.99	0
	Play Offs	1	60.00	50	8	8.00	84.00	0
	Totals	15	867.24	628	62	4.29	90.13	1
Charlotte Jackson	Cup	1	60.00	59	13	13.00	77.97	0
	League	1	60.00	38	4	4.00	89.47	0
	Totals	2	120.00	97	17	8.50	82.47	0

Netminding Break-Down – Season 2024/25

League	Netminder	GPI	Min	SA	GA	GAA	Save %	SO
@ KIN	Drinkwater	1	60	39	4	4.00	89.74	0
@ SHE	Drinkwater	1	60	33	1	1.00	96.97	0
@ WHI	Drinkwater	1	60	55	6	6.00	89.09	0
v WHI	Drinkwater	1	60	43	5	5.00	88.37	0
@ CAL	Jackson	1	60	38	4	4.00	89.47	0
@ TEL	Drinkwater	1	60	37	2	2.00	94.59	0
V TEL	Drinkwater	1	60	39	4	4.00	89.74	0
V SHE	Drinkwater	1	60	49	2	2.00	95.92	0
v KIN	Drinkwater	1	60	32	4	4.00	87.50	0
v LEE	Drinkwater	1	60	49	1	1.00	97.96	0
V CAL	Drinkwater	1	60	16	0	0.00	100.00	1
@ LEE	Drinkwater*	1	46	29	3	3.91	89.66	0
	Totals	**12**	**706**	**459**	**36**	**3.06**	**92.16**	**1**

Cup	Netminder	GPI	Min	SA	GA	GAA	Save %	SO
v SHE	Drinkwater	1	60	59	10	10.00	83.05	0
@ SHE	Drinkwater	1	60	50	7	7.00	86.00	0
v TEL	Drinkwater	1	41.3	48	5	7.26	89.58	0
@ TEL	Jackson	1	60	59	13	13.00	77.97	0
	Totals	**4**	**221.3**	**216**	**35**	**9.49**	**83.80**	**0**

Play Offs	Netminder	GPI	Min	SA	GA	GAA	Save %	SO
v STR	Drinkwater	1	60	50	8	8.00	84.00	0

Widnes Wild Women - Season 2024/25 (Photo by Wil Evans)

Back Row: Steve Furber, Katie Adshead, Grace Teinert, Jennifer Greenwood, Jennifer Hickey, Sophie Hill, Laura Moran, Karyn Cooper, Leen de Decker, Eleanor Johnson, Amanda Armstrong, Niamh Horsfield, Ruth Leopold, Natalie Buckles, Thomas Horner. Front Row: Suzie Miller, Charlotte McAdam, Elizabeth Loss, Charlotte Cramp, Stephanie Drinkwater, Rachael Pearce, Ellen Tyrer, Phoebe Patient, Lise Gillen, Victoria Connelly

Widnes Wild Women Results - Season 2024/25

Date		Home			Away	
29/9/24	D2N	Kingston Diamonds	4	4	Widnes Wild	D
12/10/24	D2N	Sheffield Shadows	1	2	Widnes Wild	W
27/10/24	D2N	Whitley Bay Beacons	6	4	Widnes Wild	L
24/11/24	D2N	Widnes Wild	6	5	Whitley Bay Beacons	W
7/12/24	D2N	Caledonia Queen Bees	4	12	Widnes Wild	W
15/12/24	Cup	Widnes Wild	2	10	Sheffield Shadows	L
12/1/25	D2N	Telford Wrekin Raiders	2	2	Widnes Wild	D
26/1/25	D2N	Widnes Wild	5	4	Telford Wrekin Raiders	W
2/2/25	Cup	Sheffield Shadows	7	3	Widnes Wild	L
16/2/25	Cup	Widnes Wild	5	5	Telford Wrekin Raiders	Da[1]
9/3/25	D2N	Widnes Wild	4	2	Sheffield Shadows	W
16/3/25	D2N	Widnes Wild	4	4	Kingston Diamonds	D
13/4/25	D2N	Widnes Wild	2	1	Leeds Roses	W
27/4/25	D2N	Widnes Wild	8	0	Caledonia Queen Bees	W
3/5/25	Cup	Telford Wrekin Raiders	13	3	Widnes Wild	L
10/5/25	D2N	Leeds Roses	3	3	Widnes Wild	Da[2]
24/05/25	POS	Widnes Wild	1	8	Streatham Storm	L

1: *Game abandoned at 41.19 due to a player injury. Result recorded as a 5-5 draw – the score at the time of the stoppage.*

2: *Game abandoned at 46.05 due to a player injury. Result recorded as a 3-3 draw – the score at the time of the stoppage.*

Wild Women Season Preview

The Widnes Wild women's team have announced their leadership teams in preparation for the new 2024/25 WNIHL season, which starts this weekend.

The Head Coach for the new season is Steve Furber, with Thomas (Paddy) Horner as Assistant Coach. Leen De Decker, Katie Fairclough and Suzie Miller will all be Player / Coaches.

Charlotte Cramp returns as team captain in the role that she filled so admirably last season and Rachael Pearce and Elizabeth Loss are Alternate Captains.

The Wild Women will, once again, be playing in WNIHL Division 2 North where they will take on opposition from: Hull, Sheffield, Whitley Bay, Edinburgh, Telford and Leeds.

Last year's strugglers Grimsby withdrew from the league during the summer and a new 3-team Northern Cup competition has been introduced between Widnes, Telford and Sheffield to provide extra matches to make up the shortfall.

The Wild Women start their season with a trip to Hull and back this Sunday 29th September when they take on the Kingston Diamonds. They then have two more away fixtures before their first home game against Whitley Bay Beacons on Sunday 24th November at Planet Ice Widnes, 4.25pm face off.

The full fixture list for the 2024/25 season is:

29th Sept: away @ Kingston
12th Oct: away @ Sheffield
27th Oct: away @ Whitley
24th Nov: home v Whitley
7th Dec: away @ Caledonia
15th Dec: home v Sheffield (Cup)
12th Jan: away @ Telford
26th Jan: home v Telford
2nd Feb: away @ Sheffield (Cup)
16th Feb: home v Telford (Cup)
9th Mar: home v Sheffield
16th Mar: home v Kingston
22nd Mar: away @ Leeds
13th April: home v Leeds
27th April: home v Caledonia
3rd May: away @ Telford (Cup)

Meet The Wild Women – 2024/25

#1 Stephanie Drinkwater: Netminder Stephanie is one of the original Wild Women players who moved to Widnes when the club was relocated from Altrincham in the wake of the Manchester Phoenix fiasco back in 2015.

She has played over 100 competitive league games in total – some 85 for Widnes – and was a member of the Wild women's team that won the Division 1 North league title in the 2019/20 season to add the title she won at Altrincham in 2014/15.

She played in 10 games last season and ended up with a very impressive Save Percentage of 90.78% and 2 shut outs. She returns for her 9th season in Widnes colours this season. .

#5 Leen De Decker. Leen is another original Wild Woman and had previously played 8 seasons for Kingston Diamonds before arriving at Widnes via Altrincham. She was, until recently, the most capped player for her native Belgium with 52 World Championship games under her belt, along with 3 WC bronze medals and 1 silver medal.

Leen has played in 7 of the Wild Women's 8 seasons – having been behind the scenes in a coaching capacity last season – and has scored 86 goals and 34 assists in 72 competitive matches. She was an important member of the Wild women's team that won the Division 1 North league title in the 2019/20 season and was team captain for the 2022/23 season when they were league runners up.

#6 Vanessa Crickmore-Clarke. Vanessa is a highly experienced attacker turned defender who won 5 league titles with the Sunderland Scorpions in her native north east and then spent 9 seasons playing at Deeside and Altrincham before the move to Widnes. Like Drinkwater and de Decker, she also won the Division 1 North title with Altrincham in 2014 and Widnes in 2020 and, in an impressive career to date, has played over 250 competitive games in total. She played in 8 games for Widnes last season.

#7: Ruth Leopold. Ruth is new face in a Widnes shirt this season but has been very well-known around the women's game for many years. She started playing for the Blackpool Blades women' team in 1987/88 and then moved to the Blackburn Falcons. She joined the newly formed Sheffield Shadows for the 1993/94 season – scoring the club s' first ever goal – then moved down to Bristol for work and joined the Swindon Top Cats in 1995. Ruth won a number of Division One titles with Swindon and also had a WPL title-winning year with Slough in 1998/99 before returning to the Top Cats and later Bristol Huskies.

Talking about joining Widnes for the coming season, Leopold said; "I moved back up to Lytham last year and thought I had retired, but was inspired by Rachael (Pearce) to come back and started training with Blackburn women. I enjoyed that so wanted to play league hockey again, and I decided to come along to Widnes. I am really looking forward to the season, where I hope my experience can be an asset to help the team. I am very grateful to the Wild for giving me a chance to continue playing the sport I have loved for 37 years!"

#8 Suzie Miller: Suzie is back for her 5th season in Widnes colours, having originally joined the Wild women for the 2019/20 title winning season. In that time she has played 42 games, contributing 4 assists from her defensive role. Behind the scenes, Suzie is also a qualified coach and manager.

#9 Natalie Buckles: Non playing coach this season.

#10 Lise Gillen: Ontario-born Lise Gillen brings a wealth of experience having played 3 seasons for the Guildford Lightning in the Womens' Elite League, as well as playing in her native Canada. She has played 14 games for Widnes over the past 2 seasons, scoring 4 goals and 6 assists

#11: Katie Fairclough. Katie first joined the Wild in 2017 and will be back for her seventh season in Widnes colours. She has gained international honours at GB Women's Under 18 level and was a league title winner with the Wild women in 2020. Last season, Fairclough was the Wild women's second highest scorer with 10 goals and 5 assists in 10 games and, overall, she has played 72 games for Widnes, scoring 39+25 with 83 penalty minutes. Katie is also a qualified coach and match official.

#12 Katie Adshead: Katie returns for her 6th season with the Wild team, having originally joined for the 2018/19 season. She has notched up 63 matches in that time, scoring 3 goals and 8 assists with 24 penalty minutes and was another key member of the 2019/20 title winning season.

#13 Rachael Pearce: Rachael is back for her 3rd season with the Wild women's team and brings a huge amount of experience, stretching back to the Blackpool women's team in the late 1980s, the Blackburn Falcons team in the early 1990s and then more recently with the Wyre Seagulls and the Blackburn Thunder women's team. She has been an "ever present" since joining the Wild Women and has scored 10 goals and 12 assists in 27 league and play off games.

#15 Laura Moran. Laura returns for her second season in Wild colours with over 80 WNIHL matches under her belt, having previously played for 8 years for the Oxford Midnight Stars in Division 2 South. She has 4 career goals and 12 assists from her defensive role and has notched up 44 penalty minutes. Moran also played University hockey for 4 seasons with the UAE (University Of East Anglia) Avalanche, scoring 1+2 in 18 games.

#18: Grace Teinert. Grace is a new player to the team, having come up through the highly respected Hockey Basics and Hockey Excellence programmes at the Widnes rink. She is a development player and this will be her first season of competitive ice hockey. Her brother Daniel is a Wild Academy junior player and her father Mike is a two time Summer Cup winner with the Riverside Raiders recreational team.

#19: Cath Thornton. Cath is a new face to Widnes fans but she played league ice hockey for the Deeside-based Flintshire Furies – alongside fellow Wild women Catherine Fell and Vanessa Crickmore-Clarke - for four seasons, scoring 7 goals and 4 assists in 48 competitive matches.

She has most recently been playing for the Connah's Quay Cobras recreational team at Deeside.

#22: Jennifer Hickey. Jennifer joined the Wild women for the 2021/22 season and has played in all 42 games that the team have played since then. She has contributed 5 goals and 6 assists and picked up just 6 penalty minutes. Hickey also plays University hockey for the Manchester Metros, scoring 7+12 in 52 games over three seasons.

#23: Ellen Tyrer. Ellen also made her Wild women's senior debut in the Women's Premier League in the 2021/22 season, having previously played for the Wild Academy Under 15 and Under 18 teams. In 38 league, play off and challenge games over her three seasons with the Wild women so far, she has also scored 8 goals and 6 assists.

#26: Niamh Horsfield. Previously played University hockey with Manchester Metros

#27: Lucy Kirkham. Lucy will be back for her 6th season as a Wild player, having originally moved with the Phoenix contingent from Altrincham in 2015 but spending the period 2018 to 2022 away from the game. She has played 51 competitive matches for the Wild Women, scoring 11 goals and 20 assists. She played in 3 games last season - and even went in goal for 20 minutes for the abandoned match away at Grimsby.

#29: Charlotte Cramp. Charlotte returns to the Wild women for her fourth season, having joined the team in 2021 from a background of university hockey with Manchester Metros. In her three seasons with the Wild to date, she has played 42 games and scored 6 goals and 14 assists. She will again be the captain of the Wild women's team for the new season, having admirably fulfilled the role last term. She is also a qualified match official.

#34: Elizabeth Loss. Experienced centre Elizabeth was one of the original Manchester Phoenix team that moved to Widnes in 2015 and, in her 7 seasons with the Wild women, has played 54 games, scoring 4 goals and 16 assists - and never picking up a single penalty minute. Liz was a key member of the Widnes team that won the 2019/20 Division 1 North league title.

#44: Phoebe Patient. Phoebe also played for the Wild Academy Under 15 and Under 18 teams and made her Wild women's senior debut in the Women's Premier League in the 2021/22 season. In 39 league, play off and challenge games over her three seasons with the Wild women so far, she has scored 5 goals and 4 assists.

#54: Charlotte Jackson. Netminder Charlotte was another member of the Wild women's team that won the North 1 league title in the 2019/20 season and also played in the 2012/22 post-Covid Premier League campaign. Since then, she has been away at Nottingham University studying for a Criminology degree and playing for the Mavericks University side. She also plays roller hockey, has represented GB in the past and won a number of tournaments with the Sirens team. Charlotte's brother, Tom Jackson, is the player coach of the Widnes Wild Moralee Division men's team.

#65: Karyn Cooper. Karyn returns for her 5th season with the Wild women, having originally joined the team for the

2018/19 season. She also played University hockey for the Manchester Metros team, clocking up 43 games in 4 years. In her 5 seasons to date at Widnes, Karyn has played in 62 league, playoff and challenge matches, contributing 7 assists. She is also the Wild women's Team Manager and puts in a huge amount of work behind the scenes.

#66: Jemma Brown. Jemma also returns for her 5th season at Widnes, having previously played for the Kingston Diamonds in the Women's Premier League as well as junior hockey for Blackburn and Trafford. She was a member of the Wild women's team that won the Division 1 North title in 2019/20 and has played 48 league and challenge matches for Widnes scoring 8 goals and 10 assists.

#68: Abigail Aldred. Abigail returns for her second season with Widnes, having played 7 games last season. In a busy year all round, she also played with the Nottingham Vipers womens team in WNIHL Division 1 and the Manchester Storm mixed Under 18 team last season. She has previously played with the Manchester Under 16 girls' team and is an assistant coach with them for this season.

#71: Amanda Armstrong. Amanda was another of the original Wild Women who moved from Altrincham in 2015 and went on to play for Widnes for 4 seasons until 2019. In an impressive career spanning over 20 years, she has played some 250 competitive games and has been Head Coach of the Manchester Storm Under16 girls' team for the past 2 seasons. During her previous stint with Widnes, she scored 15 goals and 13 assists in 39 games.

#72: Savannah Sumner. Sav was the first Widnes-born and trained player ever to play a competitive match for a Wild team when she and fellow local girl Sal Roberts took to the ice against Milton Keynes Falcons in the first game of the 2016/2017 season.

She played for the Wild Women for 4 seasons and was part of the team that won the 2019/20 Division 1 North title before moving to play for Whitley Bay in the Women's Elite League. She played 3 more games for Widnes in the 2022/23 season bringing her total in Wild colours to 48 games, scoring 18 goals and 12 assists.

#73: Catherine Fell. Catherine returns for her 8th season with the Wild Women, having been another of the "originals" who moved from Altrincham 2015.

Fell began playing hockey with the Blackburn Thunder team in the 2001/2002 season and played 6 seasons with them and 6 seasons with the Deeside-based Flintshire Furies, before joining the Manchester Phoenix Women's Team for their 2014/2015 Division 1 North winning season.

She has played 60 competitive matches for the Wild Women, scoring 20 goals and 16 assists and was a member of the team that won the league title in 2019/20.

#74: Sophie Hill. Sophie returns for her third season with Widnes. She has played 6 games in the past two seasons, scoring 2 goals and 3 assists.

#77 Jennifer Greenwood. Previously played 3 seasons with Blackburn Thunder i Division 1 North, 2004-07.

#79: Nicole Rainey. A Manchester Storm junior player who played 9 games with their U16 girls' team last season.

#88: Victoria Connelly. Victoria is back for her third season as a Widnes player. She is a former Guildford Lightning Elite player, previously playing for the Bracknell Fire Bees and has made 14 appearances for the Wild Women over the past 2 seasons, scoring 6 goals and 2 assists.

#95: Eleanor Johnson. Eleanor made her senior debut with the Wild Women last season, icing in 6 WNIHL matches. She also played for the Manchester Storm Under 16 girls' team and will be splitting her time this season between Widnes and the new Under 16s girls' team at Deeside.

#97: Charlotte McAdam. Charlotte returns for her second season in Widnes colours. Last season was her first in competitive hockey and she played in 4 games for the Wild Women.

New Wild Women signing Ruth Leopold
(Photo by Natalie Buckles)

Sunday 29ᵗʰ September 2024 – WNIHL Div 2 (N)
Kingston Diamonds 4 – Widnes Wild Women 4

The Widnes Wild women's team started their 2024/25 Division 2 North season with a 4-4 draw away to the Kingston Diamonds in Hull on Sunday.

The game saw Wild debuts for new signings Jennifer Greenwood, Ruth Leopold, Nicole Rainey and Niamh Horsfield – and returns to the team for Sav Sumner and Charlotte Jackson after spending some time away with other clubs.

The two teams were very closely matched throughout this game and the first period remained goal-less until the very last minute when Jennifer Hickey opened the scoring for the Wild with just 35 seconds left on the clock.

Two goals early in the second period put the Diamonds in the lead and they edged further ahead with a goal on 30 minutes to lead 3-1 at the second interval.

The Wild Women visibly upped their game in the third period and two goals in two minutes – from Katie Fairclough and Leen de Decker – put them on level terms with 13 minutes left to play.

Kingston got their noses back in front with a 4th goal on 50 minutes but de Decker equalised again with 4 minutes left on the clock to secure the point for Widnes.

The Wild Women have two more away fixtures - at Sheffield on 12th October and Whitley Bay on 27th October - before their first home game against Whitley Bay Beacons on Sunday 24th November at Planet Ice Widnes, 4.25pm face off.

*****

Ruth Leopold is a new face in a Widnes shirt this season but has been very well-known around the women's game for many years. She started playing for the Blackpool Blades women's team in 1987/88 and then moved to the Blackburn Falcons in 1991.

She joined the newly formed Sheffield Shadows for the 1993/94 season – scoring the club's first ever goal – then moved down to Bristol for work and joined the Swindon Top Cats in 1995.

Ruth won a number of Division One titles with Swindon and also had a WPL title-winning year with Slough in 1998/99 before returning to the Top Cats and later playing for the Bristol Huskies.

Talking about joining Widnes for the new season, Leopold said;

"I moved back up to Lytham last year and thought I had retired, but was inspired by Rachael (Pearce) to come back and started training with Blackburn women. I enjoyed that so wanted to play league hockey again, and I decided to come along to Widnes."

"I am really looking forward to the season, where I hope my experience can be an asset to help the team. I am very grateful to the Wild for giving me a chance to continue playing the sport I have loved for 37 years!"

Netminder Stephanie Drinkwater was the Wild Women's MVP away at Sheffield

Saturday 12th October 2024 – WNIHL Div 2N
Sheffield Shadows 1 – Widnes Wild Women 2

The Widnes Wild women's team continued their unbeaten start to the new season with a 1-2 win away to Sheffield Shadows on Saturday.

As the score suggests, this was a very close game and the result could have gone either way until the very last seconds.

Sheffield took the lead in the 5th minute but Widnes drew level on 10 minutes with a goal from former Belgium international player Leen de Decker. The Wild Women went ahead on 15 minutes with another de Decker strike, this time a powerplay goal punishing a Sheffield stick-holding penalty.

The score remained 1-2 at the first period break and, despite numerous chances for both sides, it also ended up as the final score.

Sheffield upped the pressure as the game progressed, looking for an equaliser forcing Widnes into taking a few defensive penalties as they battled to keep them at bay. Wild netminder Stephanie Drinkwater put in a superb performance in front of goal keeping out 32 of the 33 shots that she faced - and was named MVP for the Wild women.

The Wild Women have another away fixture - at Whitley Bay on 27th October - before their first home game of the season against Whitley Bay Beacons on Sunday 24th November at Planet Ice Widnes, 4.25pm face off.

Leen de Decker (Photo by Wil Evans)

Leen De Decker is one of the original Wild Women players who moved to Widnes when the club was relocated from Altrincham in the wake of the Manchester Phoenix fiasco back in 2015, and had previously played 8 seasons for Kingston Diamonds before arriving at Widnes via Altrincham.

She was, until recently, the most capped player for her native Belgium with 52 World Championship games under her belt, along with 3 WC bronze medals and 1 silver medal.

Leen has played in 7 of the Wild Women's 8 seasons – having been behind the scenes in a coaching capacity last season – and in that time, scored 86 goals and 34 assists in 72 competitive matches. She was an important member of the Wild women's team that won the Division 1 North league title in the 2019/20 season and was team captain for the 2022/23 season when they were league runners up.

Previous Wild Women's team sponsor Laura Prescott from Debt Movement UK (Photo by Paul Breeze)

Widnes Wild Women Seeking Sponsors

The Widnes Wild women's team are looking for sponsors to support them during the 2024/25 Womens National Ice Hockey League season.

The Wild Women are a not-for-profit women's ice hockey team with players ranging across from 14 years to 50+ years old, playing out of the Planet Ice rink in Widnes. They are playing this season in the women's Division 2 North and are hoping to make it to play offs in May for promotion to the national Division 1 for next year.

The 2024/25 season runs until the end of May and sees the Wild women travelling far and wide across the country, facing opposition from Hull, Sheffield, Leeds, Telford, Whitley Bay and Edinburgh.

There are a number of sponsorship package options, which include company promotion such as:

- Company logo on playing jerseys
- Ceremonial puck drops & MVP presentations
- Regular social media coverage
- Company announcements on match days

Another sponsorship option, which has been popular in previous years is an individual, player sponsorship. The benefits of Individual Player Sponsorship include:

- Company logo on the player's home and away jerseys
- Company name announcements at every home game, and when your player scores or is awarded MVP
- Tagged in social media posts about the player

Interested parties are requested to contact the Wild Women's team in the first instance via their Facebook page.

The Wild Women are away to Whitley Bay Beacons this Sunday 27th October, 5pm face off, and play their first home game of the season against the same opposition on Sunday 24th November at Planet Ice Widnes, 4.25pm face off.

Stephanie Drinkwater and Jennifer Greenwood defend the Wild goal away at Whitley (Photo by Mark Bird Sports Photography)

Sunday 27th October 2024 – WNIHL Div 2 N
Whitley Bay Beacons 6 - Widnes Wild Women 4

The Widnes Wild Women's team suffered their first defeat of the season with 6-4 loss away to Whitley Bay Beacons on Sunday.

The Wild Women made the long trip to the North East with a strong squad and were boosted by the return of former player coach Amanda Armstrong, who has rejoined the club after 5 seasons away from playing.

Whitley opened the scoring on 2 minutes and were 2-0 up 5 minutes later. Widnes pulled a goal back with a strike from Phoebe Patient on 15 minutes but Whitley restored the two-goal cushion heading into the last minute of the period.

A goal from Jemma Brown with just 6 seconds left on the clock narrowed the deficit again and the score stood at 3-2 at the first interval.

The Beacons made the score 4-2 with a goal 2 minutes into the second period but Widnes fought back and goals from returnee Amanda Armstrong and team captain Charlotte Cramp – on 25 and 28 minutes respectively - saw them level at the second period break.

Unfortunately, Widnes were unable to carry this momentum into the third period and two unanswered goals late in the game handed Whitley the 6-4 win.

The Wild Women are next in action on Sunday 24th November when they play their first home game of the season – again against Whitley Bay Beacons – at Planet Ice Widnes, 4.25pm face off.

Amanda Armstrong (Photo by Flyfifer Photography)

Amanda Armstrong (formerly Williams) is one of the original Wild Women players who moved to Widnes when the club was relocated from Altrincham back in 2015, and went on to play for Widnes for 4 seasons until 2019.

In an impressive career spanning over 20 years - including 13 seasons at Blackburn Thunder – she has played some 250 competitive games and has been Head Coach of the Manchester Storm Under16 girls' team for the past 2 seasons. During her previous stint with Widnes, Amanda scored 15 goals and 13 assists in 39 games

Charlotte Cramp (Photo by Mark Bird Sports Photography)

Charlotte Cramp Selected For GB Students Team

Widnes Wild women's team captain Charlotte Cramp has been selected to play for the Great Britain students' team at the World Students Games in Italy in January.

The 2025 FISA World University Games will take place in the Piedmonte region around Turin from 13th to 23rd January and will feature a variety of outdoor and indoor winter sports.

Alpine skiing, snowboarding, and freestyle will be staged in Bardonecchia, cross-country skiing, biathlon, and ski orienteering in Pragelato, and ski mountaineering in Sestriere.

The indoor sports of figure skating, short track speed skating and curling will be held in Turin and ice hockey matches will be divided around three venues - in Pinerolo, Torre Pellice and Turin.

The GB Students team will come against opposition from Canada, Chinese Taipei, Czech Republic, Japan, Kazakhstan, Slovakia, and the USA.

Talking about her GB selection, Charlotte said:

"I'm so excited to have been selected to compete in the FISU World University Games with the GB Students Ice Hockey Team. Being selected for any form of team or competition is amazing, however this opportunity is an absolute dream come true."

"I am extremely grateful and excited for the opportunity to represent GB Students in Torino, Italy in January 2025.Over the next few months I will be putting in a lot of hard work both on and off the ice to ensure I am ready for the challenges at the World University Games. Bring on Italy!"

Charlotte Cramp is now playing in her fourth season with the Wild women, having joined the team in 2021 from a background of university hockey with Manchester Metros.

In her previous three seasons with the Wild, she played 42 games and scored 6 goals and 14 assists.

She is captain of the Wild women's team for the second season in a row, having admirably fulfilled the role last term.

Charlotte is also a qualified match official and regularly officiates at Moralee and Laidler Division matches in the NIHL.

Jemma Brown was the Wild Women's MVP against Whitley
(Photo by Mark Bird Sports Photography)

Sunday 24th November 2024 – WNIHL Division 2 North
Widnes Wild Women 6 – Whitley Bay Beacons 5

The Widnes Wild Women's team won their first home game of the season by the narrowest of margins with a 6-5 victory over Whitley Bay Beacons at Planet Ice Widnes on Sunday.

This was a highly entertaining match to watch with plenty of end to end action throughout and numerous chances for both sides.

Whitley had the better of the first period, outshooting the Wild women by some 2 to 1. They took the lead in the 10th minute and were 0-2 up by the first period break.

Widnes visibly upped their game in the second period and pulled a goal back through Jemma Brown on 27 minutes, however, that was the only goal action of the second period and the score stood 1-2 to the Beacons with 20 minutes left to play.

The third period saw a veritable scoring-fest, with 8 goals being fired in, and the result remaining open to question until the very last seconds.

Whitley scored again just 34 seconds in to lead 1-3 but 2 goals within a minute of each other - from team captain Charlotte Cramp and Phoebe Patient – saw the Wild Women draw level.

Just when it looked as if Widnes would go on to take control of the match, Katie Fairclough picked up a game misconduct penalty for slashing and the Wild women had to play 5 minutes shorthanded. Despite coming under intense pressure, they managed to weather this storm with staunch team defending and netminder Stephanie Drinkwater performing heroics in the Widnes goal.

A strike from Leen de Decker on 52 minutes put Widnes ahead for the first time in the game and a second goal from Cramp just 27 seconds after that extended the home advantage. Two goals from Whitley levelled the score again but Leen de Decker fired home the winning goal with just over 2 minutes left on the clock.

The Wild Women are next in action on Saturday 7th December when they make the long journey north of the border to play the Caledonia Steel Queens in Edinburgh, 4pm face off, and are next at home on Sunday 15th December when they take on Sheffield Shadows at Planet Ice Widnes, 4.25pm start.

Charlotte Cramp at the Women's World Championship in 2024

International Calls Up For Match Officials

Three match officials with Widnes connections have been selected by the International Ice Hockey Federation (IIHF) to officiate across the world at international tournaments during the current 2024/25 season.

Charlotte Cramp is the current Widnes Wild women's team captain and she also officiates at men's NIHL Moralee and Laidler Division matches.

She has officiated at the women's playoffs weekend for the last 3 seasons, and the most recent season, did the men's Laidler Division play offs and was on the crew for the women's Elite final

This is her second year officiating at international level as she was a linesman at the Women's Under 18 World Championships Division II Group B in Sofia, Bulgaria, last year. In March, Charlotte will be officiating at the senior

Women's World Championships Division IIIA in Belgrade, Serbia.

Philippa MacKinnon (previously Wheeler) played for the Widnes women's team in the 2018/19 Women's Premier League season and also played league hockey for Peterborough and Nottingham. She officiates at NIHL Moralee Division level and has only recently returned to the ice after having a baby 4 months ago.

She was a linesman at the Youth Olympics in Switzerland in 2020, the Women's U18 World Championships in Istanbul Turkey in 2022 and again in Dumfries in 2023. In January she will be officiating at the Women's Under 18 World Championship Division III in Zagreb, Croatia.

David Good is an experienced Elite League referee who previously played as netminder for his hometown Hull Jets in the NIHL.

He was drafted in by the Wild as an emergency loan player for two games at the 2016 Laidler Division Play Off weekend after regular Widnes netminder Greg Ruxton suffered an injury late in the season.

Widnes beat Nottingham Lions 2-1 in the semi-final and lost out to league champions Deeside Dragons 5-2 in the final. As a result of this, Good has an impressive all time Widnes netminding record of 90.40 Save Percentage from his two games.

He was a referee at the World Youth Olympics in Lausanne in 2020 and the Under 20 World Championships in Iceland in 2023.

Charlotte McAdam scored her first Wild Women's goal away at Caledonia (Photo by Mark Bird Sports Photography)

Saturday 7th December – WNIHL Div 2N
Caledonia Queen Bees 4 - Widnes Wild Women 12

The Widnes Wild women's team battled through hurricane conditions to head north to Scotland but it was all worthwhile as they came home with a 4-12 victory over the Caledonia Queen Bees on Saturday.

The Queen Bees are a new team in the league this season and are a second team to the Caledonia Steel Queens, who won the league title last season and are now playing in the higher WNIHL Division 1.

The match was played at the Border Ice Rink in Kelso which the Caledonia club use quite often and, as it is a good 50 miles further south than their regular home rink of Murrayfield in Edinburgh, is a bit easier to get to.

This was the Wild women's first visit to that compact and bijou venue and it took them a while to get used to the unusual surroundings.

It was quite a close game in its early stages and the Queen Bees took the lead after just 2 minutes of play. Jemma Brown equalised for the Wild skating the whole length of the ice to do so - on 12 minutes and then Lise Gillen fired Widnes in front three minutes later.

Caledonia equalised with 2 minutes left on the clock and the score stood at 2-2 at the first period break.

Two quick goals within 45 seconds of each other at the start of the second period - from Gillen and Amanda Armstrong – put Widnes back in front and they never really looked back from there.

The Wild Women fired in two more goals – from Abigail Aldred (her first ever competitive goal), and team captain Charlotte Cramp – before Caledonia eventually pulled a goal back on 38 minutes.

Charlotte McAdam had left the game early in the first period after a hefty collision with the boards but bravely returned to the ice and was rewarded with her first Wild women's goal with 54 seconds left in the second. The score stood at 3-7 at the second interval and the Wild Women looked well in control.

Caledonia scored their 4th goal 50 seconds into the third period but any hopes of their mounting a late comeback were well and truly scotched with 5 unanswered goals - from Victoria Connelly, Gillen again for a hat-trick and three more from Cramp – handing the Wild Women an emphatic 4-12 victory.

The Wild Women are next in action this Sunday 15th December when they take on Sheffield Shadows at Planet Ice Widnes, 4.25pm face off.

In a break from the league programme, this match is part of new cup competition that was introduced for this season to make up the number of games after the Grimsby team withdrew from competing.

Alongside their league meetings, Widnes will play Sheffield and Telford once home and once away in a three team "round robin" cup group that will decided an overall winner.

*****

The Wild Women had THREE players called Charlotte in their team on Saturday – Charlotte Cramp, Charlotte McAdam and netminder Charlotte Jackson.

Please note that the goalscorer details for this report have been taken from Wild Women's team coach Paddy Horner's notes and NOT from the official gamesheet so there may be some discrepancies.

Sunday 15th December 2024 – WNIHL North Cup: Widnes Wild Women 2 – Sheffield Shadows 10

The Widnes Wild women's team had a difficult start to their WNIHL North Cup campaign with a rather unexpected 2-10 defeat at home to Sheffield Shadows at Planet Ice Widnes on Sunday.

When the two teams met in the league earlier in the season away at iceSheffield, the game had finished in a very close 1-2 win for the Wild, so this result was rather unexpected.

This is the first year that the WNIHL has run a separate cup alongside the league competition and it has been introduced for this season to make up the number of games after the Grimsby team withdrew from this season's WNIHL Division 2 North. Alongside their league meetings, Widnes are playing Sheffield and Telford once home and once away in a three team "round robin" cup group that will decide an overall winner. A separate cup competition also sees Leeds, Kingston and Caledonia meeting in a similar format.

Sheffield came out of the blocks the quickest and took the lead after just 3 minutes. They doubled their advantage three minutes later and Widnes had to wait until the 14th minute to open their own account with a goal from Katie Fairclough. The score stood at a fairly manageable 1-2 to Sheffield at the first period break with both sides very much in contention.

Two more goals early in the second period saw the Shadows edge further ahead but Fairclough found the

134

back of the net once again to bring the score to 2-4 at the second interval.

Widnes still looked in with a shout at this point but the floodgates opened up in the third period as Sheffield outshot the Wild Women by a massive 24 to 5 and their effort were duly rewarded. 6 unanswered goals swept past overworked netminder Stephanie Drinkwater in the final 20 minutes of play, helping Sheffield to a higher margin of victory than the Wild performance possibly deserved.

The Wild Women have a few weeks' break now to lick their wounds and regroup before the season restarts in January. They travel to Telford to face the Wrekin Raiders on Sunday12th January and are next at home on Sunday 26th January when they take on the same opposition at Planet Ice Widnes, 4.25pm face off.

Sunday's game saw a Widnes debut for recent signing Cath Thornton. Cath may be a new face to Widnes fans but she played league ice hockey for the Deeside-based Flintshire Furies – alongside fellow Wild women Catherine Fell and Vanessa Crickmore-Clarke - for four seasons from 2005 to 2010, scoring 7 goals and 4 assists in 48 competitive matches.

She has most recently been playing for the Connah's Quay Cobras recreational team at Deeside.

Thornton was named MVP for the Wild Women in her first game at Widnes.

The Wild Women's team enjoy their annual fancy dress Christmas scrimmage (Photo by Rachael Pearce)

Widnes Wild Women Top Of The League For New Year

The Widnes Wild women's team finish the year proudly occupying top spot in the Division 2 North league table, with 3 wins, 1 draw and 1 defeat from their 5 league games to date.

They are being stalked, however, by Leeds Roses and Telford Wrekin Raiders who are just 1 point behind and each with a game in hand, but there is still a long way to go in this year's league title chase.

It is a fascinating competition this season with no one team dominating and everybody looking capable of beating everybody else.

The only exception to this might be the Edinburgh based Caledonia Queen Bees who are a new team for this season and are a development team for the Steel Queens team who won the league last season and were promoted to Division 1. They have lost all 5 of their league games so far this season, conceding 67 goals, of which 12 came in the Wild Women's visit north of the border in early December.

Team captain Charlotte Cramp is the Wild Women's leading scorer at this early stage of the season with 7 goals and 5 assists from 5 games. Former Belgium international player Leen de Decker is second with 6+3 and recently returned Amanda Armstrong is just behind them with 3+4.

The goals and assists have been widely spread around the squad this season with Lise Gillen, Jemma Brown, Phoebe Patient, Jennifer Hickey, Victoria Connelly, Abigail Aldred, Katie Fairclough and Charlotte McAdam all having found the net and 6 other players all contributing assists.

Katie Fairclough is the current leader by some distance in the Division 2 North "Bad Girl" stakes with 31 penalty minutes, due mainly to her 5+game for slashing in the home game against Whitley.

Katie is beaten, however, in the overall Division 2 penalty standings by three there players from South 2 who all have 45 PIMs despite each having played fewer games than her.

The Wild Women are also taking part in a cup competition for the first time this season – playing Sheffield and Telford home and away in a 3-team round robin.

They lost their opening game 2-10 at home to Sheffield just before Christmas so have a bit of ground to make up if they are going to have any chance in that competition.

The Wild Women are back in action on Sunday 12th January when they travel to Telford to face the Wrekin Raiders for a league game.

Wild Women In Top Of The Table Clash

The Widnes Wild women's team will be hoping that the weather has improved enough for them to be able to travel to Telford on Sunday 12th January for a top of the table clash against the Wrekin Raiders in their first match of the new year.

The Wild women topped the Division 2 North table over the festive period but a narrow 2-1 win for Telford over Whitley Bay Beacons on Saturday saw them leapfrog them into top spot and they now head the table by 1 point, having played the same number of games.

The Wild women are then at home to Telford on Sunday 26th January at Planet Ice Widnes, 4.25pm face off.

Sunday 12th January 2025 – WNIHL Division 2 North
Telford Wrekin Raiders 2 – Widnes Wild Women 2

The Widnes Wild women's team put in a superb performance in their top of the table clash away to Telford Wrekin Raiders to come home from Shropshire with a creditable 2-2 on Sunday.

It is the first time in 4 attempts that the Wild women have ever picked up a point away to the perennial title contenders and it will stand them in good stead should the teams finish locked on points at the end of the season, when league positions are decided by results between the two teams.

Telford opened the scoring with just 18 seconds on the clock but Widnes equalised 51 seconds later with a goal from Leen de Decker and the score remained 1-1 at the first period break.

The Wild Women took the lead 47 seconds into the second period with a Lise Gillen strike and it took Telford until the 35th minute to manage a reply. There was absolutely nothing to choose between the two teams as they went into the third period at a finely balanced 2-2.

Despite numerous chances at both ends, neither side was able to break the deadlock and the game finished as a draw.

The situation at the top of the Women's Division 2 North is extremely close after the weekend's games. Telford remain top with 9 points from 6 games and Widnes are second with 8 points from 6.

Kingston Diamonds are just one point behind them and Leeds and Sheffield both follow on 6 points each.

The fascinating title battle will continue when the Wild women play host to Telford at home on Sunday 26th January at Planet Ice Widnes, 4.25pm face off.

Wild Women Aim To Top Table in Crunch Encounter

The Widnes Wild women's team have the chance to go back to the top of the WNIHL Division 2 North table this weekend as they take on current league leaders Telford Wrekin Raiders this Sunday 26th January at Planet Ice Widnes, 4.25pm face off.

The two teams drew 2-2 in a very close and nail biting encounter in Shropshire two weeks ago – the first time that the Wild womens have ever taken a point away to Telford – and they will be keen to go one better on Sunday.

A win for the Wild women would see them leapfrog the Raiders and take a narrow 1 point lead at the top. With just 2 points being awarded for a win in the women's leagues – as opposed to three for a regulation time victory in the men's NIHL – the league positions are very close with just three points separating the top 5 teams.

Telford currently lead the table with 9 points from their 6 games to date while Widnes are second with 8 points from 6 games. Kingston Diamonds have also played 6 games and are in third place with 7 points, while Leeds and Sheffield are close behind with 6 points each from 5 games played.

The Wild women previously won the league title at this level back in the 2019/20 season, when it was known as Division 1 North.

Katie Fairclough was the Wild Women's MVP in the win over Telford
(Photo by Paul Breeze)

Sunday 26th January 2025 – WNIHL Div 2 N
Widnes Wild Women 5 – Telford Wrekin Raiders 4

The Widnes Wild women's team moved back to the top of the Division 2 North table after a close-fought and highly entertaining 5-4 victory over erstwhile league leaders Telford Wrekin Raiders at Planet Ice Widnes on Sunday.

The division's top two teams had played out a fascinating chess-match like 2-2 draw down in Shropshire two weeks earlier and this game was just as nerve-wracking and finely poised - and the result could easily have gone either way right until the final seconds.

Telford took the lead in the 7th minute and, despite Widnes out-shooting the visitors by more than 2 to 1, the score remained 0-1 at the first period break.

The continued Wild pressure was eventually rewarded in the 24th minute when Leen de Decker fired in a delayed penalty goal punishing a Telford holding call.

Telford edged ahead again just 90 seconds later but the Wild Women levelled once more three minutes after that with a goal from Lise Gillen. A further Raiders goal on 35 minutes put Telford noses back in front and the score stood at 2-3 at the second interval.

The third period saw Telford on top in terms of shots on goal and they scored a fourth goal 4 minutes in to open up a two-goal lead.

Ellen Tyrer pulled a goal back for Widnes two minutes later and this sparked a late fight back by the home side. De Decker fired home on a powerplay on 52 minutes to level the score once again and the Wild took the lead for the first time in the game with Gillen's second goal of the night on 56 minutes.

The Wild women held on in the last few minutes to secure a 5-4 victory - which could be highly significant for the league title race. Having drawn the away game with Telford 2-2, this win means that, should the two teams finish level on points in the league table at the end of the season, Widnes would take the higher position based on results between the two teams.

Sunday 2nd February 2025 – WNIHL Division 2 North Cup: Sheffield Shadows 7 - Widnes Wild Women 3

It looks as if the Widnes Wild women's team will be able to "concentrate on the league" after a frustrating 7-3 cup defeat away to Sheffield Shadows on Sunday.

This is the first time that the women's league have organised a separate cup competition and the three-way tournament between Widnes, Sheffield and Telford offers additional games to pad out the regular league schedule. However, despite doing well in the league and currently topping the Division 2 North table, Widnes have struggled in the cup and lost their opening match 2-10 at home to Sheffield back in December.

The away game on Sunday was a much better performance and was closely fought for much of its duration. Widnes actually scored first, with Rachael Pearce firing home in the 3rd minute and it took Sheffield right up until the 19th minute to equalise, leaving the score at a finely-balanced 1-1 at the first period break.

The only goal of the second period saw Sheffield take the lead on 23 minutes and, despite numerous chances at both ends, they remained 2-1 ahead at the second interval.

Widnes equalised 9 minutes into the third period – some 25 minutes after the previous goal – with a strike from Leen de Decker but they were unable to push on from this breakthrough and take control of the game. Sheffield edged back in front on 50 minutes and two more goals within 77 seconds saw them open up a 5-2 lead.

Jemma Brown pulled a goal back for the Wild Women on 53 minutes but the damage had already been done and two late strikes for the Shadows gave the final score a more lop-sided look than the Widnes performance possibly deserved.

The Wild Women still have two more cup games to play – at home to Telford on Sunday 16th February and away in Shropshire on 3rd May – but even if they win both of those, the results in the games between Sheffield and Telford will probably determine the winners of this inaugural cup competition.

Sunday 16th February 2025 – WNIHL North Cup

Widnes Wild Women 5 Telford Wrekin Raiders 5

(Match abandoned at 41.19)

Cath Thornton scored her first goal for the Wild Women (Photo by Paul Breeze)

The Widnes Wild women's team saw their cup game against Telford Wrekin Raiders abandoned early in the 3rd period - with the score standing at 5-5 - after an injury to a Telford player at Planet Ice Widnes on Sunday.

The game had started well for Widnes as Katie Fairclough fired them into the lead after just 2 minutes. Telford hit back with two quick goals but a second from Fairclough on 10 minutes levelled the score again.

The Raiders edged back into the lead just two minutes later and then 2 quick fire goals within 8 seconds of each other in the last minute of the period put them 2-5 ahead.

Widnes pulled goal a back on 24 minutes with a strike from Amanda Armstrong and then a goal from Cath Thornton – her first in Widnes colours – on 29 minutes – narrowed the deficit to just one.

There followed a tense spell of end- to-end hockey with chances at both ends but it took until the last minute of the period for the next goal – which fell to the Wild's Rachael Pearce to level the score at a finely balanced 5-5.

A barnstorming third period looked to be on the cards but, sadly, it was not to be as with only 1.19 played, a Telford player suffered a heavy collision against the boards and collapsed onto the ice.

There was a significant delay while she received medical attention in–situ and, by the time that she could be safely moved from the ice, there wasn't enough ice time left to play out the remainder of the game.

The two team coaches and the match officials decided to call off the game at that point and it was officially abandoned.

According to the official England Ice Hockey regulations, in the case of a match being abandoned due a medical emergency with neither team being at fault:

"Where less than 2 periods of the match have been played, a 0-0 draw will be declared with each team being awarded one point. Where more than 2 periods of the match have been played, the result at the point of abandonment will stand."

This would suggest that the match will be recorded as a 5-5 draw, but that will still have to be decided by the League Management Committee after considering reports from the various officials involved.

The Wild Women are next in action on Sunday 9th March when they take on Sheffield Shadows in a league game at Planet Ice Widnes, 4.25pm face off.

*Ellen Tyrer was the Wild Women's MVP against Sheffield
(Photo by Suzie Miller)*

Sunday 9th March 2025 – WNIHL Division 2 North
Widnes Wild Women 4 – Sheffield Shadows 2

The Widnes Wild women's team maintained their Division 2 North league title challenge with a hard fought 4-2 win over Sheffield Shadows at Planet Ice Widnes on Sunday.

Sheffield opened the scoring after just two minutes and it took until later into the period for Widnes to open their own account. Two quick fire goals from Leen de Decker just 38 seconds apart on 17 minutes drew the Wild Women level and then gave them a slender lead going into the first break.

Another Widnes goal – from Amanda Armstrong on 22 minutes – edged the Wild Women further ahead but Sheffield pulled a goal back at the midway point of the game and the score stood at a tantalisingly close 3-2 at the second interval.

Sheffield actually out-shot Widnes by some margin, with the overall tally for the game amounting to 18 to 49 and it took an inspirational performance from Stephanie Drinkwater in the Wild goal to keep the Shadows attack at bay.

Widnes nerves were eased by de Decker's hat–trick on 50 minutes and with no more scoring after that, the Wild were able to celebrate a 4-2 victory.

The Widnes Wild Women are at home again this Sunday 16th March when they take on Kingston Diamonds at Planet Ice Widnes, 4.25pm face off.

Ruth Leopold was the Wild Women's MVP against Kingston
(Photo by Paul Breeze)

Sunday 16th March 2025 – WNIHL Division 2 North
Widnes Wild Women 4 – Kingston Diamonds 4

The Widnes Wild women's team battled hard to salvage a well deserved point in their 4-4 draw against Kingston Diamonds at Planet Ice Widnes on Sunday.

After a very nervy and close opening phase, Kingston eventually opened the scoring in the 15th minute. They scored again 60 seconds later and took a 0-2 lead into the first period break.

A powerplay strike from Lucy Kirkham 2 minutes into the second period, punishing a Kingston boarding call, pulled a goal back for Widnes but a powerplay goal for the

Diamonds just 3 minutes later restored their 2-goal advantage.

Ruth Leopold pulled another goal back for Widnes two minutes after that and then a Phoebe Patient strike on 38 minutes put the Wild Women on level terms at 3-3 heading into the third period.

Kingston edged back in front again with a goal on 48 minutes but a well-taken short handed goal from Leen de Decker tied the score for Widnes once again with 5 minutes left to play.

Unfortunately, they were unable to build, on this and the game finished in a 4-4 draw – the same score as in the away game between the two teams earlier in the season.

The Widnes Wild women's team's game that was scheduled to be played away against Leeds Roses on Saturday was postponed and will now take place on 10th May. The game will be played at Bradford due to a lack of available ice time at the Leeds rink and it will be the first time that the Wild Women have ever played at that venue.

The Wild Women's next game is at home to Leeds on Sunday 13th April at Planet Ice Widnes, 4.25pm face off.

Stephanie Drinkwater was the Wild Women's MVP against Leeds (Photo by Paul Breeze)

Sunday 13th April 2025 – WNIHL Division 2 North
Widnes Wild Women 2 – Leeds Roses 1

The Widnes Wild Women maintained their Division 2 North title challenge with a hard fought 2-1 win over Leeds Roses at Planet Ice Widnes on Sunday.

This was a very entertaining game to watch – with the result remaining in doubt until the very last seconds - and many observers agreed that it was quite possibly one of the best women's matches ever seen at the Widnes rink.

Leeds opened the scoring with a goal on 9 minutes and the score remained 0-1 at the first period break. Widnes equalised on 24 minutes with a strike from Ruth Leopold and, despite chances for both teams, the score stood at 1-1 at the second interval.

This game was end to end action throughout, although the Roses had the edge in terms of shots on goal – out-shooting the Wild Women by 49 to 36 over the whole 60 minutes. However, they came up against Stephanie Drinkwater who was in fine form in the Widnes goal and made a succession of stunning saves, keeping out an impressive 48 of the 49 shots that she faced, for a 97.96 save percentage.

Widnes eventually took the lead on 47 minutes with a first Wild goal for Jennifer Greenwood, setting up a nail-biting finale.

Despite the closeness of this game and its significance for the league standings, it was played in good spirit throughout, with very few penalties being awarded.

Just 4 minutes of penalties were handed out to each side over the course of the game and two each of these came in the third period when Widnes were defending their slender lead.

The Wild Women managed to fend off the Leeds assault when they were a player down and were unable to take advantage when the tables were turned with 6 minutes left to play.

The clock slowly ticked down and, despite a late flurry of pressure from Leeds, Widnes were able to hold on and record an important victory.

The MVP awards - sponsored this season by niche publishers Ice Hockey Review – were presented by match volunteer Lynda Bird and went to Kirsty Hodgins for Leeds and Stephanie Drinkwater for Widnes.

The Wild women now have 6 wins, three draws and one defeat from their 10 league games to date. The other teams in the mix for the league title have games to catch up on so the table standings for Division 2 are far from clear at present.

Widnes play their last home game of the season on Sunday 27th April when they take on Caledonia Steel Queens at Planet Ice Widnes. The game has a later than usual face off time of 5.45pm.

They then finish off their regular league schedule with an away game to Leeds Roses on 10th May – which will be played at Bradford Ice Rink due to a lack of available ice time at Leeds.

The Wild Women celebrate their 2020 title win
(Photo by Mo Muir)

Wild Women's Title Push – 21st April 2025

The Widnes Wild Women play their last home game of the season this Sunday 27th April when they take on Caledonia Bees at Planet Ice Widnes and their mission is clear. If they can win this game and then win their final league game away at Leeds Roses on 10th May, they will secure the Division 2 North league title.

The Wild Women currently top the Division 2 North league table with 15 points - a playing record of six wins, three draws and one defeat from their 10 games to date. There is a chasing pack of three more teams who are also still in with a chance of the title – perennial challengers Telford Wrekin Raiders, Sheffield Shadows and Leeds Roses.

Sheffield and Telford are currently vying for second place and have 14 and 13 points respectively from 10 games.

Leeds are playing catch up in the fixture list and have 2 games in hand. The good news for the Wild Women is that the Roses have games against both Telford and Sheffield over the weekend of 3rd and 4th May so it is likely that, depending on those results, one or more of those teams will be played out of the title race by the time Widnes play Leeds the weekend after.

With there only being 12 matches in the league schedule this season, the table is very tight and the title may well be decided by a single point margin or less. This works in Widnes' favour at present as teams that finish on the same number of points are separated by results in matches played between them.

With the Wild Women having beaten Sheffield both home and away and also having beaten Telford narrowly at home after a draw away in Shropshire, they would take the top spot if they were to finish on the same number of points as either of those two teams.

On paper, the home game against Caledonia should be the easier of the two games in the Wild Women's title run-in. The Edinburgh-based Bees are a new team in the division for this season and are a development team for the Caledonia Steel Queens who play in Division 1.

They are bottom of the league table, having lost all 11 of their games to date, with a goal difference of minus 81. The Wild Women beat them 4-12 when they ventured north of the border back in December.

But there is no such thing as a certainty in ice hockey and games still need to be won - so the Wild women will need to be at their very best on Sunday.

The away game at Leeds is likely to be a very different kettle of fish entirely and the Wild Women only very narrowly beat them 2-1 in the recent encounter in Widnes. Depending on the other results in the intervening period, the game on 10th May could well be a deciding "winner takes all" clash for the league title.

The Wild Women previously won the league title in the 2019/20 season. They finished second in the league in 2022/23.

Wild Women MVP Jennifer Hickey (Photo by Paul Breeze)

27th April 2025 – WNIHL Div2 North
Widnes Wild Women 8 – Caledonia Bees 0

The Widnes Wild women's team took a step closer to winning the league title with an 8-0 win over Caledonia Bees at Planet Ice Widnes on Sunday.

The Edinburgh-based Bees are a new team in the division for this season and are a development team for the Caledonia Steel Queens who play in Division 1. They arrived bottom of the league table, having lost all 11 of their previous games and the Wild Women beat them 4-12 when they ventured north of the border back in December, so this game always seemed likely to be a bit of a home banker.

The match was actually very close in its early stages and a single goal – scored by Leen de Decker on 6 minutes -

saw the Wild Women take a very slender 1-0 lead into the first period break.

A second goal for the Wild – from Ellen Tyrer just 90 seconds into the second period settled any nerves that might have been lingering and then a goal from Jennifer Hickey just 60 seconds after that put the Wild Women well and truly in the driving seat.

The score remained 3-0 at the second interval but the flood gates opened in the third period and 5 unanswered goals – from Charlotte Cramp, de Decker again, Phoebe Patient and a brace for Ruth Leopold - saw Widnes sweep to the win.

While the end result was quite conclusive, this was far from a one-sided game and the Bees put in a very good showing. They looked dangerous going forward and Stephanie Drinkwater was called upon to make a number of spectacular saves to secure a first shut out of the season.

The MVP awards - sponsored this season by niche publishers Ice Hockey Review – were presented by match volunteer Lynda Bird and went to Lily Taylor for Caledonia and Jennifer Hickey for Widnes.

The win means that Widnes remain top of the Division 2 North table with 17 points from 11 games. With title rivals Leeds Roses beating Kingston Diamonds 3-0 at the weekend, the run-in for the league championship remains very tight. Leeds have games in hand to play and need to win them all if they are to have any chance of overtaking Widnes. The two teams meet in their last game of the league season - in what may well be a title decider - in Bradford on 10th May.

The Wild Women in celebratory mood (Photo by Wil Evans)

Wild Women Are Champions!

The Widnes Wild Women's team secured the Division 2 North league title after a fascinating weekend of ice hockey saw their rivals for the crown knock each other out of contention.

Widnes actually lost their own game 13-3 away to Telford on Saturday - but that was a cup game and had no bearing on the outcome of the league, which as it turned out, was decided by results elsewhere.

The Wild Women went into the weekend leading the D2N table with 17 points from their 11 league games – and one match still to play, away to Leeds Roses on 10th May.

Sheffield Shadows were in second with 14 points from 10 games and could still snatch the title if they won their remaining games and Widnes lost away at Leeds. Leeds themselves were also still in the running with 11 points from 9 games, knowing that 3 wins in their last 3 games could possibly see them overtake Widnes on the last day of the season

Somewhat fortuitously for the Wild Women, the fixture list pitched Leeds and Sheffield up against each other in Leeds on Saturday night, with the Roses winning 5-2. That result meant that Sheffield could no longer overtake the Wild Women at the top of the league table, even if they won their last remaining game.

Leeds, however, could still snatch the title if they won their two remaining matches and could beat Widnes in the last game of the season on 10th May.

Telford – who are perennial title challengers themselves but have dropped off the pace a little this year - did the Wild Women a huge favour by holding the Roses to a 2-2 draw in Shropshire on Sunday night meaning that Leeds are now also unable to deny Widnes top spot.

The weekend results mean that the Wild Women take the league title irrespective of what happens in the remaining games of the regular season.

They have also qualified for the end of season play offs, which take place over the Bank Holiday weekend of 24th to 26th May in Sheffield, where the top 2 teams in Division 2 North will compete with the top teams from Division 2 South for promotion to Division 1 for next season.

Karyn Cooper scored two goals at Telford and was named Wild Women's MVP (Photo by Flyfifer Photography)

Saturday 3rd May 2025 – WNIHL North Cup
Telford Wrekin Raiders 13 – Widnes Wild Women 3

The Widnes Wild Women lost their final game in the WNIHL North Cup 13-3 away to Telford Wrekin Raiders on Saturday.

In competitive terms, this game was a bit of a dead rubber as neither team could win the cup, having both already lost twice to Sheffield Shadows, who are the other team in this three-way tournament, but pride was still very much on the line.

The earlier cup game between these two teams had ended in a 5-5 draw in Widnes after being abandoned early in the third period due to a player injury and with the two league meetings both going the way of Widnes - with a narrow 5-4 win at home and a 2-2 draw away in

Shropshire - Telford probably felt they had a point to prove.

Telford took the lead in the 7th minute but Widnes equalised just 60 seconds later with a goal from Catherine Fell.

Telford edged back in front on 13 minutes but a strike from Karyn Cooper – her first ever goal for the Wild women - on 16 minutes levelled the scores once again. However, the Wild Women were unable to build on this and two more goals late in the period gave Telford a 4-2 lead at the first break.

The damage was all done in the second period when Telford fired in 7 goals before Widnes were able to summon up a reply. A second goal of the game from Cooper with just 3 seconds left in the period gave the travelling contingent something to cheer about but, with the score standing at 11-3 at the second interval, the game was already well and truly over as a contest.

Telford eased their foot off the gas in the third period - quite possibly saving some energy for their league encounter with title challengers Leeds Roses the following night - and the game finished as a 13-3 win for the Raiders.

Despite the one-sided scoreline, Charlotte Jackson put in a good performance in the Widnes goal, turning away an impressive 46 of the 59 shots that she faced over the 60 minutes.

Karyn Cooper was named MVP for the Wild Women after her two goal haul having played up front instead of in her usual defensive role in a make-shift playing line-up.

Jemma Brown scored the first Widnes goal at Leeds and was named MVP for the Wild Women (Photo by Paul Breeze)

Saturday 10th May 2025 – WNIHL Div2N
Leeds Roses 3 – Widnes Wild Women 3
(Match Abandoned 46m)

The Widnes Wild women's team saw their league title winning season come to a rather subdued end after their final game away to Leeds was abandoned midway through the third period due to a player injury.

The score stood at 3-3 at the time and, subject to official confirmation, that is likely to be recorded as the final result.

While it is always nice to win, the result of this game didn't really matter too much to the Wild Women as they had already accrued enough points to secure the league championship.

Leeds, however, really needed to win to have a chance of finishing in second position in the league and clinching the remaining play off place.

Player injuries and match abandonments aside, it was a fascinating end to the season as three teams went into the final weekend level on 14 points – Leeds, Telford and Sheffield - any of whom could have finished in the runners up spot.

The game at Leeds – as the result suggests - was very close. It took until the 15th minute for the deadlock to be broken and a Jemma Brown goal fired the Wild Women into the lead.

40 seconds later it was 0-2 to Widnes after a strike from Lise Gillen and the score remained 0-2 at the first break.

Gillen found the back of the net again 4 minutes into the second period to put Widnes 0-3 up but then Leeds began to fight back.

They pulled a goal back just 70 seconds later and then further narrowed the deficit at the midway point of the game. The score stood at a tantalisingly close 2-3 at the second interval and Leeds went on to draw level on 44 minutes.

Unfortunately, we will never know what might have happened next as the game was called to a halt shortly after that.

Draws are fairly rare in ice hockey – especially in recent seasons since many leagues have adopted overtime and penalties shots to decide tied matches.

However, assuming that Saturday's game remains a draw, it will mean that the Wild Women have had an incredible FIVE draws from their 16 games this season.

They drew 2-2 away at Telford in the league, drew 4-4 both home and away against Kingston Diamonds and then saw their home cup game against Telford also end in a 5-5 draw, another game that was stopped early due to a player injury.

The draw away at Leeds means that Widnes finish top of the Division 2 North table with 18 points from their 12 league games.

With Leeds only drawing on Saturday, this meant they finished the league campaign on 15 points. Sheffield beat Whitley Bay Beacons 7-2, also on Saturday, and thus finished their season on 16 points putting them above Leeds and in the driving seat for the runners up spot – at least overnight.

The matter was eventually settled on Sunday when Telford Wrekin Raiders hammered Kingston Diamonds 17-0 to match the Shadows on points but secure second place with a superior goal difference of +41 to +26.

As things turned out, the point that Leeds dropped in the abandoned drawn game wouldn't have been enough to send them to the playoffs anyway as Telford would still have come out on top of the chasing pack due to the way that the league separate teams that have finished level in the table.

Wild Women at the Play Offs in 2017 (left to right): Sav Sumner, Sophie Sinclair Reeks, Tegan Lavery, Abigail Hayes, Beckie Elliott, Leen de Decker, Lucy Kirkham, Katie Hills, Sarah Roberts & Emma Pearson. (Photo by MyTeamPhoto.com)

Wild Women Off To Play Offs

The Widnes Wild women's team head to Sheffield at the weekend to take part in the Women's National Ice Hockey League (WNIHL) Play Offs, which will run over 3 days and feature 13 games in total.

As champions of Division 2 North, the Wild Women will take on Streatham Storm (2nd team), who finished second Division 2 South, in their semi final - giving them a, possibly, slightly easier match than if they had finished second themselves and then had to face D2S champions Cambridge.

They will play in the second semi final, which faces off at 8.15pm on Saturday evening. The other semi final sees Telford take on Cambridge with a 6pm start time. The Division 2 final is at 2.45pm on the Sunday and the winner will secure the Play Off title as well as promotion to Division 1 for next season.

The other games over the weekend see the semi finals and final for the Division 1, the Women's Elite League and the Girls' Under 16 championship, as well as the promotion / relegation match between the winners of the D1 final and the bottom team in the Elite League.

This is the Wild Women's 4th trip to the play offs. On each previous occasion, they have bowed out at the semi final stage and have never yet got through to the final.

They reached the Play Offs two seasons running in their early years when they were in the Women's Premier League (now called WNIHL Division 1). They were runners up in the league in 2015/16 and narrowly lost 2-1 to Streatham Storm (1st team) in the play off semi final and finished 4th in 2016/17, losing to the same opposition again 6-1.

The Wild Women won the Division 1 North league title (which is now the equivalent of Division 2 North) in the 2019/20 season and qualified for the play offs once again, but they never took place because of the Coronavirus pandemic.

They came second in the third tier in the 2022/23 season and lost 3-1 in the play-off semi final to D2S champions Cardiff, so will be hoping to go one better this time around.

Wild Women Division 2 North champions
(Photo by Stewart Cutting)

Saturday 24th May 2020 – WNIHL Play Off Semi Final
Widnes Wild Women 1 – Streatham Storm 8

The Widnes Wild women's team put in a battling performance in their Play Off semi final at iceSheffield on Saturday, ultimately losing out 1-8 to Streatham Storm – but they, at least, had something to celebrate as they were presented with the trophy and medals for winning the Division 2 North League championship.

The Wild Women arrived at the Play Offs missing a few regular players and also had to contend with being the last game of the day, which didn't face off until 8.15pm. Streatham were a bit of an unknown quantity as WNIHL North and South teams don't usually play each other, although Widnes had played the Storm's first team a few times back in their Women's Premier League days.

As it turned out, the game was fairly even in its early stages with the two sides cautiously testing each other out. Just as it looked as if the first period would play out goal-less, Streatham fired in a goal to take the lead just 41 seconds from the buzzer. 73 seconds into the second period, the score was 0-2 to the southerners and on 25 minutes they went 0-3 ahead.

Widnes eventually found the back of the net themselves on 29 minutes with a goal from Leen de Decker, who picked up the puck behind the Storm goal and guided it around inside the right hand post – but that was about as good as things got for the Wild Women. Although they pushed forward, trying to build on this, Streatham scored again 4 minutes after that and the score remained 1-4 at the second period break.

The Widnes net bulged once again 34 seconds into the third period and, with Streatham leading 1-5 by then, the game was pretty much over as a contest. The Wild Women had their chances but were kept out by a stubborn Storm defence. This led to their own goal being put under intense pressure and only a string of impressive saves from Wild netminder Stephanie Drinkwater kept the score from being higher than it was.

The pressure continued, however, and three goals in the latter stages of the game handed Streatham a convincing 1-8 victory.

With Telford Wrekin Raiders also losing 8-1 in their semi final to Division 2 South champions Cambridge Kodiaks, this set up an all-south final on Sunday, which Cambridge went on to win 4-1.

After Saturday's semi-final, the Wild Women were presented with the league championship trophy for their

Division 2 North title win and the players were all given commemorative medals. This was an extra special moment for the Widnes team as the last time they won the league title - back in 2020 - the playoffs were cancelled due to the coronavirus pandemic, and the presentations were never made.

The Wild Women have their end of season presentation evening this weekend and can then enjoy a few weeks' break before preparations begin for the new 2025/26 WNIHL season.

The Widnes Wild Women's players outside the play off venue iceSheffield (Photo by Stewart Cutting)

Ruth Leopold, Rachael Pearce & Vanessa Crickmore-Clarke with championship medals (Photo by Stewart Cutting)

For the sake of completeness, the full list of the WNIHL Play Off weekend results were as follows:

Saturday 24th May
D1 SFinal 1: Bristol Huskies 2 – Caledonia Steel Queens 1
D1 SFinal 2: Kingston Diamonds 1 – Swindon Topcats 4
Elite Semi Final 1: Solihull Vixens – Guildford Lightning 1
Elite Semi Final 2: Queen Bees 7 – Whitley Bay 2
Division 2 Semi Final 1: Cambridge Kodiaks 8 – Telford Wrekin Raiders 1
Division 2 Semi Final 2: Widnes Wild Women 1- Streatham Storm 8

Sunday 25th May
Under 16 Semi Final 1: Chelmsford Rattlesnakes 10 – Manchester Storm 1
Under 16 Semi Final 2: Whitley 5 – Bristol 1
Division 1 Final: Bristol Huskies 3 – Swindon Topcats 2
Division 2 Final: Cambridge Kodiaks 4 – Streatham Storm 1
Elite Final: Solihull Vixens 0 - Queen Bees 2

Monday 26th May
Under 16 Final: Chelmsford 4 - Whitley 3
Elite v Div 1 Relegation Match: Kingston Diamonds v Bristol Huskies

Stephanie Drinkwater with head coach Steve Furber
(Photo by Ellen Tyrer)

Wild Women's Presentation Evening

The Widnes Wild Women's team rounded off their successful Division 2 North title winning season with their annual awards evening at the weekend.

The player awards for the 2024/25 season were:

Best Defence: Jennifer Greenwood
Best Forward: Ruth Leopold
Most Improved Player: Eleanor Johnson
Coaches' Player Of The Season: Stephanie Drinkwater
Players' Player Of The Season: Stephanie Drinkwater
Unsung Hero: Rachael Pearce

Ruth Leopold had actually retired from playing after an impressive 37 year career with Blackpool, Sheffield, Swindon and Bristol but was tempted back onto the ice after a year away to play for the Wild Women this season.

She summed up her feelings thus: "Thank you so, so much to all at Widnes Wild Women's ice hockey team for such an enjoyable season. To get a league winners medal (and hat!) - and to top it off with an unexpected Best Forward award - and some very kind words from the coaches at the end of season do tonight, was amazing and emotional for me! I appreciate it so much."

As well as being named Coaches' Player and Players' Player of the season, inspirational netminder Stephanie Drinkwater was the first inductee to the Wild Womens' 100 Club, which has been newly set up to celebrate various playing milestones.

Drinkwater passed 100 appearances for the Wild Women this season – the first player on the team to do so.

She has been with the Wild Women since the team first started 10 years ago following its relocation from Altrincham. This season is actually her third title win overall as she also won the Division 1 North title (as it was then called) with Widnes in 2020, and with the previous Manchester Phoenix team in 2015.

In that time, Drinkwater has notched up 104 appearances for the Wild Women, and it would probably have been more had the league not been suspended for the 2020/21 season due to the Coronavirus pandemic.

Hot on her heels in the "Appearances Stakes" are two more original Wild Women and triple title winners, Catherine Fell with 92 games and Leen De Decker with 91.   De Decker was also inducted into the 100 Club for having passed 100 goals for the team. She has 104 goals from her 91 games, and her tally of 46 assists and 150 points overall are also the all time highs for the Wild Women.

Talking about her hat-trick of accolades, Stephanie Drinkwater said:

"What an end to this year's season. I am lost for words after receiving Coaches' Player and Players' Player awards last night! Also being inducted into the 100 Club with officially playing 100 games for the Wild Women. It has been an amazing year and I have so much love for this team - forever my girls!"

The Wild Women now have a few weeks' well-earned rest before they return to the ice to prepare for the 2025/26 WNIHL season.

They are always keen to attract new players – especially anybody with league or international experience - and anybody interested is asked to contact the team via their Facebook page in the first instance.

Eleanor Johnson with Assistant coach Paddy Horner (Photo by Ellen Tyrer)

Wild Women Player Appearances 2015-2025

	Player	GP	G	A	Pts	PIM
1	Drinkwater, Stephanie	104	0	0	0	6
2	Fell, Catherine	92	22	33	55	60
3	De Decker, Leen	91	104	46	150	10
4	Fairclough, Katie	83	44	27	71	114
5	Cooper, Karyn	78	2	13	15	12
6	Adshead, Katie	77	3	8	11	28
7	Crickmore-Clarke, Vanessa	72	3	1	4	26
8	Loss, Elizabeth	66	4	5	9	2
9	Marcroft, Laura	64	7	10	17	6
10	Brown, Jemma	62	13	12	25	20
11	Kirkham, Lucy	61	11	20	31	4
12	Hickey, Jennifer	58	6	12	18	8
13	Miller, Suzie	57	0	4	4	2
14	Sumner, Savannah	56	25	17	42	36
15	Pearson, Emma	55	30	33	63	79
16	Cramp, Charlotte	54	15	20	35	0
17	Williams, Amanda (also Armstrong)	50	22	20	42	6
18	Patient, Phoebe	47	9	6	15	8
19	Tyrer, Ellen	46	10	10	20	4
20	Pearce, Rachael	44	12	19	31	22
21	Skilander, Danielle	43	9	10	19	2
22	Gennoe, Preston	37	37	19	56	46
23	Chapman, Charlene	37	14	11	25	10
24	Hayward, Pauline	36	0	2	2	4
25	Sinclair-Reeks, Sophie	35	3	5	8	12
26	Elliott, Beckie	34	2	3	5	2
27	Hills, Katie	31	31	19	50	54
28	McPhee, Charlotte	30	2	0	2	0
29	Hayes, Abigail	29	3	3	6	20
30	Bowen-Fell, Megan	26	1	2	3	96
31	Garner, Kathryn	25	4	6	10	8
32	Buckles, Natalie	25	1	1	2	8
33	Gillen, Lise	23	12	8	20	4
34	Connelly, Victoria	22	7	6	13	12
35	Aldred, Abigail	22	2	2	4	10
36	Boyle, Samantha Joann	22	0	1	1	8
37	Wilson, Olivia	22	0	1	1	0
38	Jackson, Charlotte	22	0	0	0	0

39	Johnson, Eleanor	21	0	3	3	2
40	Martin, Emma (also Downe)	19	2	3	5	0
41	Moran, Laura	19	0	1	1	10
42	Lloyd-Hazlegreaves, Daisy	18	1	2	3	4
43	Roberts, Sarah	18	0	1	1	8
44	Holt, Shannon	17	1	2	3	2
45	Green, Ellie	17	0	0	0	0
46	Venables, Victoria	16	1	5	6	16
47	McAdam, Charlotte	16	1	2	3	0
48	Leopold, Ruth	15	4	1	5	4
49	Hill, Sophie	14	2	2	4	0
50	Wright, Elizabeth Amy	14	0	3	3	14
51	Walsh-O'Neill, Ellie	14	2	0	2	2
52	Aspinall, Sarah-Louise	13	6	5	11	2
53	Wheeler, Philippa	13	2	3	5	4
54	Greenwood, Jennifer	12	0	1	1	2
55	Moran, Josie	12	0	0	0	0
56	Culshaw, Abigail	11	10	6	16	6
57	England, Pamela	11	0	0	0	0
58	Gustavsson, Madeleine	10	1	3	4	0
59	Oliver, Katya	9	3	5	8	2
60	Green, Sophia	8	1	5	6	12
61	Middleton, Emma	8	0	2	2	0
62	Boyle, Jodie Alexandra	8	0	0	0	0
63	Winstanley, Daisy	7	0	1	1	0
64	Fairbairn, Rachel	7	0	0	0	0
65	Horsfield, Alice	7	0	0	0	0
66	Duncan Jakki	6	0	2	2	2
67	Holliday, Katherine	4	0	0	0	0
68	Horsfield, Niamh	4	0	0	0	0
69	Cartwright, Rachel	3	2	1	3	0
70	Hutchinson, Sarah	3	0	2	2	4
71	Thornton, Cath	3	1	0	1	0
72	Bevan, Emma	3	0	0	0	0
73	Donnelley, Rebecca	3	0	0	0	0
74	Kerr,Kaitlin	2	2	2	4	2
75	Lavery, Tegan	2	0	0	0	0
76	Scott, Rebekah	2	0	0	0	0
77	Wilde, Rebecca Jade	2	0	0	0	0
78	Fletcher, Penelope	1	0	0	0	0
79	Rainey, Nicole	1	0	0	0	0

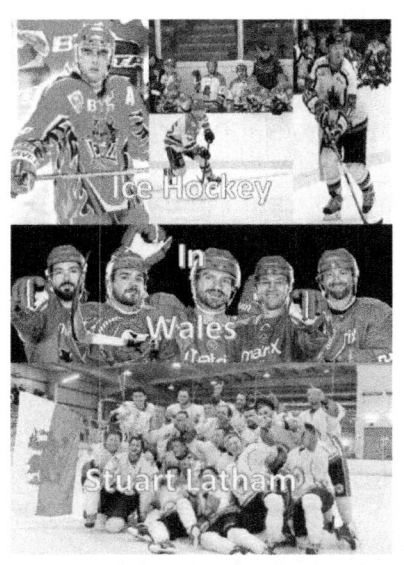

BOOK REVIEW
"Ice Hockey In Wales"
by Stuart Latham

(Originally published on icehockeyreview.co.uk on 15th February 2025)

Well – what can I say?

Stuart Latham has done it again – with another huge book about British ice hockey - this time all about "Ice Hockey in Wales".

Now, if you are a regular reader of my previous random ramblings on this subject (did you notice my double alliteration of the r-words there…?), you will know that I have already gone on at great length about the huge-ness of his previous Manchester ice hockey book "On Thin Ice" (that's the one that you couldn't read while riding no-handed on a bike – no, please, don't try that yourself - it would be reckless and dangerous, and I only mention it for historical context)…

Well, this latest offering - "Ice Hockey In Wales" - comes from the same stable, and it really is pretty much what it says on the tin. Although you couldn't creosote your fence with it in authentic Karate Kid style, you would certainly know a lot more about the subject matter than the average unassuming oriental martial arts tutor by the time you have finished reading this fascinating book.

As with all of Stuart's other ice hockey books, this one is packed with interesting facts, league tables, players stats

179

and personal stories from people who have been involved with the clubs concerned.

From a Deeside point of view, we have the various incarnations over the years of the Deeside Dragons, there is also the Flintshire Freeze who operated in the ENL in Deeside instead of the Dragons from 1998 to 2012 and an interesting piece by current Dragons GM Shaun Bebbington about the post-Covid period return of ice hockey in Deeside.

There is also a wealth of information about the Deeside second teams, covering the historical Deeside Demons, the short lived Dragons 2 and a very well written and informative (ahem…) piece about the new Deeside Ducks team that just started this season.

There's no mention of the Clwyd Flames, unfortunately, who were the Deeside second team for a couple of seasons in the early 1980s, although – to be fair - detailed information about them is pretty hard to track down.

The other ice hockey venue in Wales – down in the Welsh capital - gets similar treatment and we have year by year league tables, player stats, stories and photos (as available) about Cardiff Devils, Cardiff Rage, Cardiff Capitals, Cardiff Fire, Cardiff Fire 2, Cardiff Bears, Cardiff Satans and the new Cardiff Canucks team.

If you are a keen collector of ice hockey books in general - and Stuart Latham's books in particular - you will probably have come across a lot of this material before as he has previously produced separate volumes about the Deeside Dragons (in 2020) and Cardiff Devils (2021) but, even so – it's nice to have all this stuff together in one tidy edition and with everything brought right up to date.

So, if you want vital statistics, I'll give you some vital statistics. "Ice Hockey In Wales" is a whopping 630 pages in length - not quite as huge as "On Thin Ice"s 734 pages but it is still a heavyweight hardback.

In fact, it weighs 1.25kg, is 260mm high, 180mm wide and has a spine width of 38mm and it will stand bold and proud on your bookshelf next to the rest of your Stuart Latham ice hockey book collection.

For orders, drop Stuart a line via Facebook or send him an email to stuartlatham65@sky.com

- and get him to tell you about his other books as well.

LUCY
POET IN
RESIDENCE

"Lucy Match Scorer" caricature by
Manga Mark

BOOK REVIEW

"On Thin Ice"
By Stuart Latham

(Originally published on icehockeyreview.co.uk on 25th June 2024)

ON THIN ICE

THE INCREDIBLE RISE AND FALL
OF ICE HOCKEY IN MANCHESTER

STUART LATHAM

When I was a young lad growing up in Stanground - which, if you don't happen to know it, is a pleasant leafy suburb of the historic cathedral city of Peterborough – I once saw a very odd sight which has stayed in the back of my mind all these years.

I was walking to the sweet shop when I saw a chap – maybe late teens / early 20s (when you are 9 or 10, everybody else just looks "old" to you...) – ride by on a bike. BUT he was riding no-handed and reading a book at the same time.

Now, this was back in the mid 1970s in the days when the liberal consensus and permissive society and everything else were all in full swing and nobody had ever heard of "Health & Safety" but even then, I figured this might have been a bit of a dangerous thing to do.

As far as I can remember, he had a small paperback book balanced against the handlebars held loosely in position by his thumbs, so may well have had a modicum of control over his machine, but he certainly wasn't looking where he was going.

I don't know who he was, where he was going or what happened later – he could have come to a sticky end a bit further up the road for all I knew – but the vision of this bloke on this bike with this book has always stuck with me.

So – why am I telling you this? Well, not that I would EVER encourage or condone anybody attempting to doing anything quite so dangerous and illegal on a public road, putting themselves and others in harm's way, and however clever this particular bloke was with reading books on bicycles, I bet that he would NOT have been able to do it with Stuart Latham's new publication "On Thin Ice" – which is a fascinating comprehensive account of ice hockey in Manchester from 1961 onwards.

I have commented before on the "huge-ness" of some of Stuart's other books – the Alloa Athletic one still lays stubbornly where I first put it down because it is too heavy for me to pick up and put away anywhere - and this is another very impressive example of literary huge-ity. It is certainly too big to prop up against the handlebars and read while you are pedalling along.

If you want facts and figures to back up this assertion – or "stats", as we like to call them in the ice hockey world – I will give you some.

"On Thin Ice" has a whopping 734 pages and weighs 1.3kg! It is a hardback, which gives it that nice classic quality feel and, as the spine is 4.5cm wide, it will stand nicely on your bookshelf without falling over or flopping. It is 26.5cm tall – which is actually 1cm taller than most of Stuart's other B5 format ice hockey books – but that just means that it is easier to find on the shelf in the dark.

Now, if you are a keen collector of ice hockey books in general - and Stuart Latham's books in particular - you will probably have come across a lot of this material before as he has previously produced separate volumes about the Altrincham Aces, Manchester Phoenix and Manchester Storm teams but, even so – it's nice to have all this stuff together in one tidy edition.

This book goes right back to the early days when the original Devonshire Road rink in Altrincham first opened and boasts such well known names of the day as Chick Zamick and Art Hodgins on the Aces bench.

We then navigate through the Trafford Metros era of the late 1980s and early 90s, the first Manchester Storm team in the Superleague, the Manchester Phoenix period from 2002 to 2017 and finish up with the modern Storm and Aces teams.

As you'd expect from a Stuart Latham publication, it is packed with league tables, stats and photos. There are loads of player profiles and some great memories from people who were involved, such as

Daryl Lipsey, Hilton Ruggles and John Lawless (Storm)

Neil Morris, Tony Hand and Peter Hagan (Phoenix)

Tom Revesz, James Ashton and Sarah Hutchinson (Aces)

and there's even a bit from me in there as well…

So, there we have it: "On Thin Ice – The Incredible Rise And Fall Of Ice Hockey In Manchester".

BOOK REVIEW

Gone But Not Forgotten

(Originally published on icehockeyreview.co.uk on 20th December 2024)

I have said, in the past, that you can "never have too many ice hockey books". And, while I WOULD say that because I do, occasionally, sell the odd one or two to help fund my Twiglet habit, this book is not one of mine.

Yep, just when I was wondering how I was going to cope over the festive period without any NIHL hockey to watch or report on (we in the lower reaches don't have Boxing Day games etc like the "Elite" boys and National Division do...) this latest offering from the fine stable of Stuart Latham ice hockey club histories has landed on the doormat.

"Gone But Not Forgotten" is an interesting book as it covers a number of different teams from different eras.

Depending on how old you are and how much you might have read about past glories in British ice hockey, you may have heard of a lot of these teams already, but it is nice to see so much information all gathered up in one place.

And what we have here covers:

Kensington Corinthians (1930s)

Richmond Hawks (1930s)

Earls Court Royals (1930s)

Grosvenor House Canadians (1930s)

Wembley Canadians (1930s)

Wembley Monarchs (1930s & 40s)

Wembley Vets (1970s)

London Phoenix Flyers (Richmond – 1970s)

Richmond Flyers (1980s)

Earls Court Rangers (1930s & 40s)

London Lions (1920s & 30s)

London Lions (1970s - exhibition team)

Wembley Lions (1930s, 40s & 50s)

Milton Keynes Kings (1990s & 00s)

Ashfield Islanders (1980s & 90s)

Bournemouth Stags (1980s & 90s)

As you'd expect with a Stuart Latham compilation, the book is packed with league tables, player statistics and fascinating photos and is bound to be of interest to ice hockey fans of all the various eras.

Now if I were being picky here, (picky – moi? shurely not...) - but if I WAS being picky, I would have expected the 1980s London All Stars team (Dave Richards, Bob Mitura et al) to be worthy of a page or two in this as well. Ice hockey fans of a particular vintage may well recall that they won the 1984/85 British League Division 2 South title.

That was quite an achievement for them because – like Ashfield Islanders - they had to play all of their games away for double points, as their home ice at the Sobell Centre in Islington wasn't suitable for playing league matches.

There was, actually, quite a lot of that went on during those halcyon Heineken-fuelled "expansion" days of the mid 80s – check out Brighton and Hastings as well (oops! - he hasn't included them, either...)

But I am not being picky today. The last train to Picky-Ville has departed "ohne mich" - so I won't mention any of them...

Anyway, despite that, this book is all very interesting and represents a very good record of a lot of teams that have fallen by the wayside over the years.

So, there we have it: "Gone But Not Forgotten.

To order your copy, drop Stuart a line via Facebook or send him an email to stuartlatham65@sky.com - and get him to tell you about his other ice hockey books as well.

MORE ICE HOCKEY BOOKS BY STUART LATHAM

ISBN	Title	RRP £
9781838116507	60 Years Of The Altrincham Aces	£15.99
9781838116521	Ice Hockey in Bristol	£15.99
9781838116538	The Deeside Dragons	£15.99
9781838116545	The Manchester Storm	£15.99
9781838116569	The Rise and Fall of the Manchester Phoenix	£15.99
9781838116590	The Cardiff Devils	£16.99
9781838332808	Ice Hockey Memories	£18.99
9781838332822	The History of the Slough Jets	£17.99
9781838332846	More Ice Hockey Memories	£17.99
9780953060863	Blood Sweat and Tears Ice Hockey in Peterborough	£24.99
9780953060870	Swindon Wildcats 1986-2016	£22.99
9780953060887	The History of the Bracknell Bees	£24.99
9781838332853	Ice Hockey in Edinburgh	£18.99
9781838332891	Stars Wars - The Oxford City Stars	£16.99
9781838460907	Swindon Ice Hockey Statistically Speaking 1986-2021	£17.99
9781838460914	In Their Own Words - Swindon Ice Hockey Memories	£16.99
9781838460938	Hockey in Haringey	£17.99
9781838460952	Ice Hockey In Solihull	£18.99
9781838460983	The NHL IN The UK	£19.99
9781915697042	Ice Hockey In Guildford	£21.99

Available by mail order from Waterstones.com, brownbfs.co.uk, foyles.co.uk and other major outlets.

**For more details, contact
stuartlatham65@sky.com or tel: +44 7702035951**

ICE HOCKEY BOOKS
by Michael A Chambers

THE COMPLETE WORKS: Compendium of the Nottingham Panthers Ice Hockey Team

This is the third book on the Nottingham Panthers and is an extension to the two previous about the club with additional statistics and facts. It is an update of the recent seasons 2007-08 to 2022-23 and is filled with lots of player pictures or events not published before.
Also a complete list and register of every player to have put on the Panthers jersey from 1946 – this has never been documented until now.
It's a complete history of all of the competitions in all the seasons. Cartoons, drawings and more.

300 Pages A4 Paperback - ISBN: 979-8365711198

UK ICE HOCKEY
Its History & Competition Winners

Michael A Chambers

UK ICE HOCKEY - *Featuring:*

History of English & Scottish Leagues, Season By Season League Tables, Cup And Play Off Competitions,

Full Lists of Title & Trophy Winners, UK clubs in European Competitions, Great Britain National Team, All Star Teams

226 pages A4 paperback - ISBN: 978-0-9539398-4-8

ICE COLD MURDER –

an ice hockey murder mystery

ISBN: 978-0953939831

When a body is found within hockey owner Mark Atkin's establishment, Inspector Dilley has to unravel this terrible scene in order to find out what happened. Amongst a complexity of doors, keys and camera pictures which have much to do with it all.

Many people have much to do with the events that occur this day which puts them 'in the frame' within this much troubled club. Who did it?

Copies available from the author. Contact Michael via e-mail at: spikc2004@yahoo.co.uk

DEESIDE DUCKS
Season 2024/25

Full Contents List:

From The Editor

Pre-Season Ducks News

2024/25 Season Reports

The Ducks' Debut Season In Figures

Season Review

Player Gallery - A to Z

Ducks Miscellany

Team Staff, Off Ice Officials and Volunteers

Shirt Designs

Social Media Graphics

Bookshelf

The fascinating story of the Deeside Ducks' first – and only - season in the NIHL Laidler Division, as told in the Flintshire & Wrexham Leader newspaper and on the Ice Hockey Review website.

ISBN: 9781909643680

Available by mail order from www.poshupnorth.com, Amazon, icehockeyreview.co.uk and other quality outlets

FYLDE FLYERS
A Complete Record

The Fylde Flyers ice hockey team only existed for two seasons but they reignited interest in a sport that has a proud history in Blackpool dating back to the 1930s.

Their legacy goes on even though the team does not.

Here is the fascinating story of the Fylde Flyers.

Full Contents List:

Acknowledgements
About The Author
Historical Timeline
The SubZero Story
The "Small Ice Rink" Dilemma

2011/12 Season Summary
News Stories, Match Reports & Gamesheets
End Of Season Awards

2012/13 Season Summary
News Stories, Match Reports & Gamesheets
End Of The Line For Flyers

Fylde Flyers Fact File
Summary Of Player Statistics
Most Points
Most Goals
Most Assists
Most Appearances
Most Penalties
Netminder Statistics
Summary Of All Time League Results

Player Directory A - Z

ISBN: 9781909643130

Available by mail order from www.poshupnorth.com, Amazon, icehockeyreview.co.uk and other quality outlets

10 YEARS IN THE WILD
2013 to 2023

10 YEARS

In The Wild

Season summaries, articles, photos and statistics for the Widnes Wild NIHL team from 2013 to 2023 With all-time Player A to Z and 10-Year Playing Record

ICE HOCKEY REVIEW

Full Contents List:

Introduction

New Ice Rink Opens In Widnes

Widnes Wild Team Launch

How It All Began!

Widnes Wild's First Ever Game

Richard Charles Looks Back At The First Widnes Game

Craig Williams And The First Ever Widnes Wild Goal

Season by Season: 2013/14, 2014/15, 2015/16, 2016/17, 2017/18, 2018/19, 2019/20, 2020/21, 2021/22, 2022/23

10 Year Records

Roll Of Honour

Playing Record

Wild Player Top 10s

Head to Head Playing Records

Wild Player A To Z

Pukka Penguin

Team Staff, Off Ice Officials & Match Volunteers

Long Service Awards

Wild Shirt Retirements

NIHL Player Award Winners

Lucy London – Poet In Residence

Bookshelf

To celebrate the 10th anniversary of the founding of the Widnes Wild ice hockey team, we thought we'd gather up all the material that we have collected over the years and put it together in one single volume.

ISBN: 978-1-909643-54-3

Various mail order options available
Visit www.icehockeyreview.co.uk for more details

RAPTORS, EAGLES & HAWKS 2 TOO...

The fascinating story of "second string" national
league ice hockey in Blackburn 1991-2020

**The fascinating story of "second string"
national league ice hockey in Blackburn
1991-2020**

ISBN: 978-1-909643-63-5

Full Contents List:

Introduction

Ice Hockey Arrives In Blackburn

1991-93: Blackburn Falcons

1993-97: Blackburn Seagulls

1997-98: Blackburn Phoenix

2007-12: Lancashire Raptors
Introduction
Season By Season
All Time Player Records

2012-17: Blackburn Eagles
Season By Season
All Time Player Records

2017-20: Blackburn Hawks 2
Season By Season
All Time Player Records

Overall Playing Record
– All Teams

A to Z Players Records
– All Teams

Bookshelf

Please note: the full colour version is available direct from the publisher via
eBay. A budget black and white version is available via Amazon. Apart from
colour photos, the actual content is the same in both versions.

Mail order links can be found on
www.icehockeyreview.co.uk

Interesting Books...
...Fascinating Subjects!

www.poshupnorth.com

Check out our audio and video archive in our dedicated "Paul & Lucy's Best Kept Secrets" YouTube channel at www.youtube.com.

Printed in Dunstable, United Kingdom

64134635R00117